RESTORING THE KINGDOM OF HAWAII

RESTORING THE KINGDOM OF HAWAII

THE KANAKA MAOLI ROUTE TO INDEPENDENCE

BY

FRANCIS A. BOYLE

CLARITY PRESS, INC.

ISBN: 978-0-9860731-7-5

In-house editor: Diana G. Collier
Cover: R. Jordan P. Santos
Artwork for goddess Pele (backcover): Arthur Johnsen

Clarity Press, Inc.
Ste. 469, 3277 Roswell Rd. NE
Atlanta, GA. 30305 , USA
http://www.claritypress.com

TABLE OF CONTENTS

"Oh, honest Americans, as Christians hear me for my downtrodden people! Their form of government is as dear to them as yours is as precious to you. Quite warmly as you love your country, so they love theirs. With all your goodly possessions, covering a territory so immense that there yet remain parts unexplored, possessing islands that, although new at hand, had to be neutral ground in time of war, do not covet the little vineyard of Naboth's, so far from your shores, lest the punishment of Ahab fall upon you, if not in your day, in that of your children, for "be not deceived, God is not mocked." The people to whom your fathers told of the living God, and taught to call "Father," and now whom the sons now seek to despoil and destroy, are crying aloud to Him in their time of trouble; and He will keep His promise, and will listen to the voices of His Hawaiian children lamenting for their homes."

Her Majesty
Queen Liliuokalani

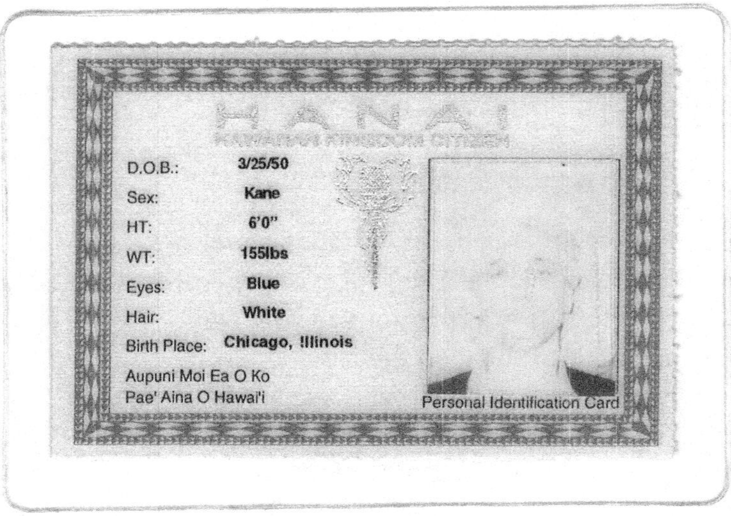
HANAI
HAWAIIAN KINGDOM CITIZEN

D.O.B.: 3/25/50
Sex: Kane
HT: 6'0"
WT: 155lbs
Eyes: Blue
Hair: White
Birth Place: Chicago, Illinois

Aupuni Moi Ea O Ko
Pae' Aina O Hawai'i

Personal Identification Card

Both sides of the author's Hawai'ian Kingdom Citizen Personal Identification Card, dated December 29, 1993. Hanai indicates that he became an Hawai'ian Kingdom Citizen by means of the traditional Kanaka Maoli custom of Adoption.

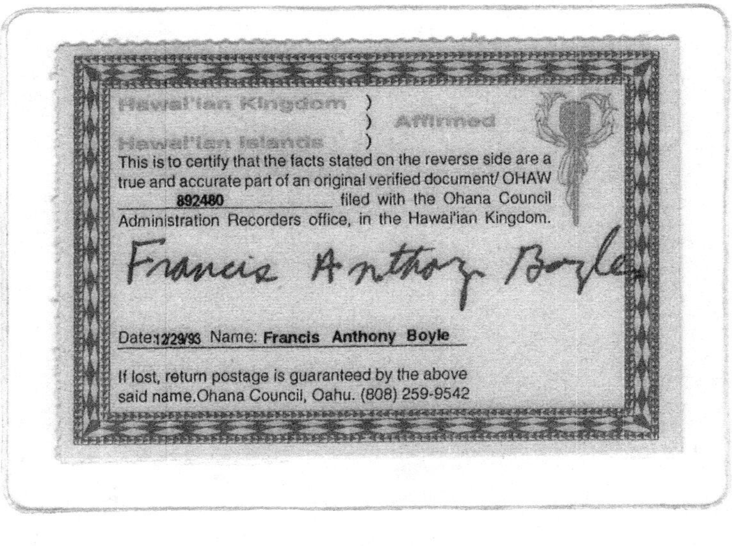
Hawai'ian Kingdom)
) Affirmed
Hawai'ian Islands)

This is to certify that the facts stated on the reverse side are a true and accurate part of an original verified document/ OHAW 892480 filed with the Ohana Council Administration Recorders office, in the Hawai'ian Kingdom.

Francis Anthony Boyle

Date 12/29/93 Name: Francis Anthony Boyle

If lost, return postage is guaranteed by the above said name.Ohana Council, Oahu. (808) 259-9542

International lawyer Francis A. Boyle (far left) on the floor of the World Court in 1993, squaring off against his adversary, Shabtai Rosenne (far right) of Israel representing Yugoslavia, just before he argued and then won the first of his two World Court Orders for Bosnia on the basis of the 1948 Genocide Convention.

INTRODUCTION

What follows is an edited version of an October 2008 interview I gave to Mr. Kuhio Vogeler as part of the research on his Ph.D. Dissertation entitled ***Prolonged Occupations: Hawai'i and the Baltic States*** *for the University of Hawaii.*

INTRODUCTION TO THE KANAKA MAOLI

Q: In school what were you taught about the United States' relationship to Hawaii?

A: Actually, I had already studied this as part of my Ph.D. dissertation at Harvard and had studied the theft of the Kingdom of Hawaii by the United States. I was familiar in a general sense with what had happened. The U.S. government illegally overthrew the Kingdom and then stole Hawaii. I was familiar before I got involved in the issue itself.

Q: So that was part of your doctorate degree or as part of getting it?

A: Actually, back in high school I had done a detailed study on the history of U.S. imperialism from the Spanish-American War into the 1920s. I studied what was done to Hawaii. I was familiar with the situation. I did not study it in great detail but I knew enough to figure out Hawaii was stolen.

Q: That paper is online, yes?

A: The high school paper? No. It later became part of my book *Foundations of World Order,* which was half of my doctoral dissertation at Harvard.[1] The genesis of that book went back to the high school paper. In the *Foreword*, I thank my high school history teacher for helping me study this imperial era of American foreign policy.

Q: Growing up, what did the media tell you about the relationship between the United States and Hawaii?

A: What the media still tells you today: that Hawaii is still a part of the United States, that it is the 50th state, and all that propaganda.

Q: Growing up, did you learn about the relationship between the United States and Hawaii from any other sources?

A: No. This was an advanced placement history course and the paper was a year-long paper. I made a very detailed study of the history of American imperialism starting with the Spanish-American War in 1898. The overthrow of the Kingdom was in 1893, but the U.S. used the Spanish-American War as a pretext to annex Hawaii in 1898. I was familiar with what had happened. I studied more since that time; but I was certainly not as familiar with all the details as when I was retained by the Hawaiian Sovereignty Advisory Commission in 1993 to give an *Opinion* on the right of the Kanaka Maoli to set up their own independent state. The impetus for that paper was President Johnson's illegal invasion of the Dominican Republic in 1965. That sparked my interest in studying the history of American imperialism going back to the Spanish-American War, and in the course of that looked into what had happened to the Kingdom of Hawaii.

Q: Did you ever visit places outside of U.S. control? And did these visits, did they lend any insight into the relationship between Hawaii and the U.S.?

A: The first time I was in Hawaii was in 1990, but that was on an anti-war court-martial at Kaneohe Bay for a Marine Corps Corporal who was the first resister to Gulf War I.[2] What really did force me to acquire a lot more detailed insight was when in 1992 the American Indian Movement set up an International Tribunal to prosecute the U.S. government for genocide, for inflicting crimes against indigenous peoples in America. They asked me to serve as the Prosecutor in light of the 500th anniversary of Columbus's invasion of the Americas. As a result of that, the American

Indian Movement invited the Kanaka Maoli to send a delegation to the Tribunal. They did so under the chairmanship of my friend, Dr. Kekuni Blaisdell. So I did argue before the Tribunal that the United States government had inflicted genocide upon the Kanaka Maoli and the Tribunal agreed with me unanimously on that point. That was the start of my personal as opposed to my academic involvement in Hawaii.[3]

That was October of 1992. Then a year later in 1993 the Hawaiian Sovereignty Advisory Commission, one of the Commissioners, Bumpy Kanahele, contacted me and asked if I would be willing to come out and give an *Opinion* on the right of the Kanaka Maoli to establish an independent state. I agreed to do that. So the next time I went to Hawaii was specifically to deal with the Native Hawaiian situation. I set aside a week for this in late December of 1993 because I told Mr. Kanahele that I wanted to go out to the different islands and meet his people on the ground; to see how they lived; to talk with them; and to evaluate their situation.[4] I really had no direct personal experience prior to that trip. You can look at the Nation of Hawaii website, or just *Google* under my name, and you can find the *Affidavit* that I submitted in Mr. Kanahele's case detailing these events and my first visit to Hawaii ....[5]

By the way, you are also asking the question on the Baltics. I grew up on the south side of Chicago and was fully aware of the tragic plight of the Lithuanians since so many people living on the south side were Lithuanian. In fact, my Aunt was Lithuanian. In 1991, when President Landsbergis declared independence and President Gorbachev set tanks on the Parliament, I did volunteer my services to President Landsbergis free of charge.[6] I had never been to Lithuania. But the south side of Chicago was like Little Lithuania and I had known what had been done to them as well as to Latvia and Estonia.

Q: Did you go out there?

A: No. I worked with them through their Ambassador Stasys Lozoraitis in the United States, starting from January 1991 through after their independence. And then Landsbergis decided not to run again. So Ambassador Lozoraitis ran for their Presidency. He lost and the people voted into power the former Communists. I have not had any contact with the Lithuanian Government since then. But I did do a great deal of legal work for them *pro bono publico* during that time.

Q: At one time, did you believe that the Hawaiian Islands were part of the U.S.?

A: Well, certainly, as a kid growing up I believed that it was the 50th state of the Union as of 1959. But once I had started to study the situation in high school, I realized that the United States had stolen the Kingdom of Hawaii; destroyed the Kingdom; stolen its land; inflicted near genocidal conditions on its people, etc.

Q: At that time, did you think that the U.S. would remain in Hawaii throughout your lifetime?

A: I cannot say I really thought about it one way or the other because I was not actively involved in the Hawaiian sovereignty movement. I just chalked it up as another example of U.S. imperialism like the invasion of the Dominican Republic or the Bay of Pigs Invasion of Cuba or the theft of Puerto Rico. I also go down to work in Puerto Rico with the Puerto Ricans to help them.[7] So how long it would last, I had not thought about one way or another. But it was clearly stolen.

Q: When did you learn that Hawaii was occupied or do you believe that Hawaii is occupied right now?

A: Sure it's occupied. Since 1893. It has been under the illegal, colonial, belligerent occupation of the United States since then. I did not study the laws of war until I went to Harvard Law School. My teacher, Richard R. Baxter, was an expert on the laws of wars. So I began to study the laws of war, belligerent occupation and things of that nature as of 1974.

Q: Was it then that you realized that Hawaii was occupied or when did you realize this?

A: I really organized my thoughts on Hawaii when the Hawaiian Sovereignty Advisory Commission invited me to come out there and give them a public lecture. I am a lawyer. I work on problems as they come along to me. It was only when I was invited to give the public lecture and to spend the next morning answering the questions by the Commissioners that I began to formally turn my area of expertise, international law, laws of war and things of that nature, to the situation in Hawaii.

Q: What was your first reaction when you started doing your research and you were ready to come out to Hawaii and you realized that: "Heh, Hawaii is occupied, this is a belligerent occupation, violating the laws of war?"

A: You can read all that in my lecture in Mable Smyth Hall.[8] There it is, spelling out the consequences for the Native Hawaiians.

Q: Did your views of the world change, or of the U.S. or understanding of yourself, did any of that change?

A: One reason the Hawaiian Sovereignty Advisory Commission retained me is that I had worked with the Palestinians in setting up the Palestinian state. Because of that experience, they wanted my position on what, if any right, did the Native Hawaiians have to do the same thing. I had been through this type of situation with the Palestinians.[9] It was nothing new. Nothing surprised me about the U.S. government. I had been studying American foreign policy since back to the Cuban Missile Crisis of 1962. Having lived through that and been threatened with extermination, it had concentrated my attention. The Cuban Missile Crisis, the Bay of Pigs, the Vietnam War, the U.S. invasion of the Dominican Republic -- nothing surprised me.

Q: As far as you know, did the number of people who understood that Hawaii is occupied increase, remain the same, or decrease?

A: Well, certainly after my lecture the people in the audience, and the people in Hawaii began to understand these issues. I presented a formal legal *Opinion* as to their situation. To the best of my knowledge, it was the first time an international lawyer had gone out there and done that. As I said, I was retained formally by the Hawaiian Sovereignty Advisory Commission, which was set up by the State of Hawaii. They paid my expenses and a modest honorarium. The check was signed by Governor Waihee, a Native Hawaiian himself. I made a Xerox of that check. I thought it was pretty cosmic to be paid by the State of Hawaii to explain why Native Hawaiians had the right to take back Hawaii and set up their own state.

Q: Did some people believe that Hawaii was different than the other states in the U.S.?

A: When I got out there, Mr. Kanahele and his group, his Ohana, the Ohana Council, the Trask Sisters and their organization, and Dr. Blaisdell were of that conviction. Already Native Hawaiians did not believe that Hawaii should be part of the United States. But they did not have the legal training that I had to articulate those arguments. Again that is why

Francis A. Boyle next to Bobby Castillo, Executive Director of the American Indian Movement, speaking at a press conference for the San Francisco Tribunal in October 1992.

Francis A. Boyle speaking out for Lithuania, Latvia, and Estonia before a rally held at the University of Illinois Quadrangle on Captive Nations Day 1991.

I was retained by the Native Hawaiian Sovereignty Advisory Commission of the State of Hawaii to come out there and give that *Opinion* which was in the lecture.

Q: Those people who think that Hawaii is the 50th state, did you have conversations with those types of folks?

A: Yes, every time I am out in Hawaii. They are the same type of people as in the former Soviet Union who believed that Lithuania was part of the Soviet Union. Lithuanians never saw it that way. In the work I did for President Landsbergis, I went back and read all the treaties for the Republic of Lithuania with the Soviet Union. If you read these treaties, it is clear that Lithuania never signed any treaty giving up its independent existence as a state and was always careful to preserve its existence as the Republic of Lithuania even under the most brutal occupation possibly imaginable under Stalin and Molotov. The Soviet Union shipped 200,000 Lithuanians off to Siberia never to emerge again. Outright genocide.

The situations are roughly analogous. The Soviet Union insisted for years that Lithuania was part of the Soviet Union. No one accepted that. Everyone knew Lithuania was independent starting with 1919 and was illegally conquered and annexed by Stalin in 1939. The haoles[10] out in Hawaii are like the Stalinists. I was over in the Soviet Union in 1989 and arguing Lithuanian independence as well. I got some Soviet lawyers to agree with me, finally, when Gorbachev admitted that there was a secret protocol to the Ribbentrop-Molotov Pact carving up Lithuania, Estonia, Latvia, and Poland between Nazi Germany and Stalinist Russia. I argued that point in the Soviet Union in 1989 when I was invited over there to lecture.

Q: What political groups have been actively trying to end the occupation?

A: You have Kanahele's group, the Nation of Hawaii. Kekuni Blaisdell. The Trask Sisters. Those are the groups that I worked with primarily over the years, and there are differences of opinion among them. There are other groups as well. I have been back to Hawaii twice since then, travelled all around and met many of the organizations, groups, individuals, and Kupunas. They are all over Hawaii. You have to go out there and find them and talk to them. The ones that I worked with closely are Kanahele, the Trask Sisters, and Kekuni.

Q: And you mentioned the argument at the Supreme Court with Keanu Sai and those folks.[11]

A: Yes, I worked with Keanu Sai and he is going back to school. He still gets involved but is not as actively involved as he used to be. He still speaks out. He started to get a Ph.D, and has somewhat retreated from activist work. But before he decided to get his degree, he was in the vanguard. I have great respect for him as well.[12]

Q: Do you believe these groups, any of these groups, have been effective?

A: Sure they have all been effective. They have turned around the debate in Hawaii. You talk with any Native Hawaiian and they all say they are entitled to sovereignty and they are all entitled to get their land back. For fifteen years I have been involved with this movement myself. You have to understand that this tragedy was inflicted by the U.S. in 1893, 115 years ago, and it is not going to be solved tomorrow. Look at Lithuania. In 1939 the Ribbentrop-Molotov Pact was followed by the illegal invasion and annexation of Lithuania by the Soviet Union. It was not until early 1990 that Landsbergis proclaimed independence and by late 1991 when the Soviet Union collapsed, Lithuania was free. We are talking about 50 plus years for Lithuania. It is a long process.

If you look at it historically, it took that many years from 1939 to 1991 for Lithuania. It will take from 1893 until I do not know when for Hawaii. Eventually it will happen. For the same reasons. The point is this, under international law, the essence of Sovereignty is a people living on their own land and asserting their own rights and that is what the Native Hawaiians are doing as we speak. This is what happened in Lithuania, Latvia, and Estonia. It happened in Palestine. I believe it will happen in Hawaii.[13]

Q: As far as you can remember, did pressure from other countries cause changes within Hawaii?

A: Before the overthrow of the Kingdom of Hawaii, there were large numbers of other countries that had diplomatic relations with Hawaii. I know Keanu Sai and several people are trying to reestablish diplomatic relations with some of them. It is obviously political because they do not want to irritate the U.S.

Q: A very good point. I have talked with a few folks who have mentioned work that has been done outside of Hawaii. It is difficult. Was there a moment when you understood that the U.S. occupation of Hawaii will end, that the U.S. government and military will leave?

A: Just based on my experience with Lithuania, I think it is mostly analogous. I know after Gorbachev sent the tanks to storm the parliament, it was a desperate situation. We were not sure what was going to happen, and working on the worst case possible scenarios that you can think of. Out of nowhere, the Soviet Union collapsed and Lithuania was free. I told this story repeatedly in Hawaii. If Lithuania can resume its independence, Hawaii can too. It is the way historical forces are working.

I can't predict the future but I have worked with the Palestinians on the creation of their state. Today the state of Palestine is recognized by 127 other states; they have de facto relations with most of Europe. They have all the rights of U.N. member states except the right to vote. The only thing keeping Palestine from being a regular member state of the U.N. is the threat of the U.S. veto. They proclaimed their state on November 15, 1988. I was their Legal Advisor, and did all the legal work on that project.[14] All the same processes are at work here. It is inevitable and everyone knows that. It will take time because the overthrow was 1893 and it is now 2008 and I can't say how long it will take.[15] But the Native Hawaiians are not going anywhere and they are not giving up.

Q: As far as you know, what factors have to change so that the U.S. government could no longer control Hawaii?

A: It is the non-consent and the opposition of the Native Hawaiians themselves. That will make it clear. It is really for them to do it for themselves. I am only an advisor and give them representation. They have to do these things themselves and there are leaders already there. I have acted through them, and I don't mean to exclude others that I met and have a lot of respect for. I am not in charge of the timetable, they are. It will be up to them to decide and to let the U.S. know that it is time for them to go home. One thing I have pointed out, and if you read my Mable Smyth lecture, is that Native Hawaiians really need to study how Gandhi conducted the struggle in India and learn from his technique, *Satyagraha*, truth-force, which I argued in 1993, was similar to *Aloha* in Hawaii. Applying *Aloha*, I felt the Native Hawaiians could throw the U.S.

out of Hawaii, just as Gandhi threw the British Empire out of the Indian subcontinent.

Again, they have to decide this for themselves and do it themselves. Nobody else can do it for them. I only give advice; what they do is up to them. You have to take a tour of Mr. Kanehele's village in Waimanalo and see what he and his people are doing in terms of building their state from the ground up. That is what they are doing. They are educating their people, reviving their language and culture and religion. And they are making their state. That is what they have to do to make it.

Q: This question is unique because you can answer it in two ways. You helped out in the Baltic States as well. As the occupation ended, did you participate in the reestablishment of the independent Baltic governments?

A: I did large numbers of position papers for the Republic of Lithuania on these types of issues, from shortly after Landsbergis proclaimed independence until after the collapse of the Soviet Union. I have many files dealing with the many problems that would confront them. However, the people then voted the former Communists back into power afterwards so I never heard back from the Republic of Lithuania. I have had no further contact since then.

Q: I have a few more questions here. You are so unique because you helped out with both. Did the ending of the occupation affect issues relating to language, culture, or ethnicity?

A: Yes, those are serious issues. I did do a Memorandum for the Republic of Lithuania. Clearly, they did a better job in protecting the basic human rights of the ethnic Russian population than happened in Latvia and Estonia. Of course there the Russian populations were higher because of the genocide and the colonialism. But the presence of other ethnic groups poses a serious problem. You have to respect the basic human rights of the ethnic Russian population of Lithuania and the native Lithuanians have tried to do so. There have been diplomatic communications back and forth. Second you do not want to irritate Russia to give them a pretext to return. I did do work on these matters.

Mr. Kanahele did ask me to do a draft of the Constitution for the Nation of Hawaii, trying to figure out how to deal with the haoles who might remain in a restored Kingdom.[16] You might want to look at that. I have had to deal with these kinds of issues for the Palestinians. I was the Legal Advisor for the Palestinians at the Middle East negotiations from 1991 to 1993 and had to deal with those types of matters including Jewish settlers remaining in the Palestinian state. I have dealt with these issues there and elsewhere.

Q: As far as you remember, how did the ending of the occupation affect real estate?

A: I have not worked on that issue in Lithuania. I did do a Memorandum for them on suing the Soviet Union at the World Court on their compensation claims for the occupation and genocide. Lithuania has not done it. I have dealt with that issue for Mr. Kanahele. It is in the draft Constitution, how we decided to handle that. You can look at it there. In Lithuania, once the former Communists were elected into power, I was dropped like a hot potato. I was not getting paid by President Landsbergis, so it did not bother me.

Q: Was there a moment that led you to believe that the Baltic States were free again?

A: It was clear with the collapse of the Soviet Union; it was a miracle from heaven. Here we were fighting to keep Lithuania alive and all of a sudden the Soviet Union collapsed. They were free!

Q: How did you feel?

A: It was great, wonderful. It was remarkable to see. I actually have a little photograph here in my office. We had a rally here on Captive Nations Day for Lithuania and Latvia and Estonia in 1991. I was speaking at the rally there with their flags. It was a wonderful experience. I was fully aware of what happened at a young age, had studied their history, growing up on the south side of Chicago.

Q: In Hawaii, have you experienced anything like that?

A: After my Mable Smyth lecture, if you see the *Affidavit* I submitted for Mr. Kanahele, you can see that he and his people, the Ohana Council, proclaimed independence.[17] And they are moving in that direction. Keanu

Sai is moving that direction. Dr. Blaisdell is moving in that direction. The Trask Sisters, they have another approach, but still are moving to establish sovereignty as they see it. I am encouraged but I can't predict the future. You can see the Palestinians. They are moving in the same direction. When I first started working with the Palestinians, no one believed they were going to have their state. But now everyone believes they will have their state eventually.

Hawaiian independence is not a case of secession. Similarly, the Soviet Union never had title to Lithuania in the first place. It is not like the attempt of the American South to secede in the civil war. Hawaii is not seceding from the United States. The United States has to pick up and go home as did the Soviet Union pick up and leave Lithuania.

Q: Back then there were two superpowers, now there is just one.

A: It looks like the United States might be collapsing as well.

Q: It is an odd thing going on in Hawaii. You actually have some Hawaiians that are not favorable to looking at Hawaii in terms of international law.

A: Most of them do. I have been all over the islands and have met repeatedly the Kupuna,[18] on almost all the islands. Most pretty much agree with the analysis that I bring to bear.

Q: They view Hawaii as being colonized. They are uncomfortable with these topics of international law, and some Hawaiian academics they feel this discussion of international law goes contrary to Hawaiian values.

A: I do not know why. The Kingdom of Hawaii had participated in the system of international law as it existed from the creation of the Kingdom to the overthrow. They had diplomatic relations all over the world, and entered into treaties. They behaved then as do what we today are calling states, and acted in the international system. I do not see how the present use of international law—effectively asserting their right to return to what they were doing before 1893—could be seen as against their interest.

One other point: the Supreme Court in Hawaii just rendered a decision on the Native Hawaiian Apology Resolution and they agreed with what I had to say in 1993: that the U.S. apology had the force of law.[19] Of course, the State of Hawaii has now appealed, hoping that the U.S. Supreme Court will overturn the Hawaii State Supreme Court.[20] Well okay. But the significant point is that they pretty much agreed with what I was saying in 1993 about the meaning and significance of the resolution.

Q: Thank you so much.

Immediately after Soviet President Mikhail Gorbachev ordered the Soviet Army to use military force against Lithuania on January 13, 1991 to suppress their independence movement, I volunteered my services free of charge to their heroic President Vytautas Landsbergis. I was then asked to put out a public statement on their behalf that was circulated all over. The relevance of Lithuania's independence movement to the Kanaka Maoli independence movement is explained in more detail in Chapter 6 below.

Public Communiqué on Lithuania

President Mikhail S. Gorbachev has violated the Kellogg-Briand Pact of 1928 and the United Nations Charter by violently suppressing the three independent states of Lithuania, Latvia and Estonia. The Kellogg-Briand Pact obligates all contracting parties to renounce war as an instrument of national policy. Lithuania, Latvia, Estonia, and the Soviet Union are all parties to this pact.

Pursuant to the infamous Ribbentrop-Molotov Pact of 1939 and its secret protocols, the Soviet Union violated the Kellogg-Briand Pact by annexing the fully independent Baltic States in 1940. Last year these three republics one-by-one, reasserted their independence and rights of self-determination under the United Nations Charter, as well as declaring the Soviet Army a force of occupation under the international laws of armed conflict and humanitarian law. President Gorbachev has now used that force to suppress the fundamental human rights and legal rights of the Baltic peoples under the Universal Declaration of Human Rights. President Gorbachev has also attempted to illegally reannex the three independent Baltic States in violation of the Kellogg-Briand Pact and the United Nations Charter. These purported reannexations are null and void under basic principles of international law, the United Nations Charter, and the Nuremberg Principles.

I call upon all states of the world community to refuse to recognize these illegal and criminal annexations of the independent Baltic Republics. These reannexations are just as illegal, reprehensible and criminal as Saddam Hussein's annexation of Kuwait. I also call upon all states of the world community to continue to recognize the independence and freedom of Lithuania, Latvia, and Estonia and their peoples as sovereign states.

I fully agree with the President of Lithuania, Vytautas Landsbergis, that President Bush has sold out Lithuania and the Baltic States to Communism and the Soviet Union, in order to promote his criminal war against Iraq. Both President Bush and President Gorbachev should be held fully accountable under the Nuremberg Principles by an international tribunal and their own peoples and parliaments, for the commission of Nuremberg Crimes Against Peace, Crimes Against Humanity, and War Crimes, as well as violations of the Geneva Conventions of 1949 and its two Additional Protocols of 1977.

I also call upon both the American people and Congress as well as the Soviet people and Parliament to impeach and remove from office Presidents Bush and Gorbachev for their heinous offenses under international law, their own constitutions, and domestic laws! Long live the *Peoples* of Lithuania, Latvia, Estonia, the United States of America, and the Soviet Union.

Francis A. Boyle
Professor of International Law
The University of Illinois College of Law
504 East Pennsylvania Avenue
Champaign, Illinois 61820
U.S.A.
January 18, 1991

ENDNOTES

1 Francis A. Boyle, Foundations of World Order (1999). The first half of my dissertation was published as Francis A. Boyle, World Politics and International Law (1985).

2 Francis A. Boyle, Protesting Power: War, Resistance and Law 117-158 (2008).

3 *See* Chapter 1 *infra*.

4 *See* Chapter 2 *infra*.

5 *See* www.hawaii-nation.org/boyleaff.html.

6 *See* Francis A. Boyle, *Public Communiqué on Lithuania* (Jan. 18, 1991) *infra* this Introduction.

7 *See* Francis A. Boyle, *Puerto Rico and the Puerto Ricans Versus 115 Years of Yankee Imperialism and Colonialism*, Global Research News, Sept. 22, 2013 *and* CounterCurrents.org, Sept. 22, 2013.

8 *See* Chapter 2 *infra*.

9 Francis A. Boyle, Palestine, Palestinians and International Law (2003) *and* Breaking All the Rules (2008).

10 Foreigners.

11 *See* Chapter 4 *infra*.

12 *See* David Keanu Sai, Ph.D., UA MAU KE EA, Sovereignty Endures: An Overview of the Political and Legal History of the Hawaiian Islands (2011).

13 *See* James Podgers, *Greetings from Independent Hawaii*, 83 American Bar Association Journal, June 1997, at 74.

14 On November 29, 2012 the United Nations General Assembly officially recognized Palestine as a United Nations Observer State. *See* Dennis Bernstein, *An Interview with Professor Francis Boyle*, Counterpunch.org, Dec. 4, 2012.

15 *See* Chapter 6 *infra* for the latest update on Palestine.

16 *See* Chapter 3 *infra*.

17 *See* Chapter 3 *infra*

18 Revered Elders.

19 Jerry Burris, *Apology Bill Has Force of Law*, Honolulu Advertiser, Feb. 2, 2008. *See* Chapter 2 *infra*.

20 *Office of Hawaiian Affairs v. Hous. & Cmty. Dev. Corp. of Haw.,* 177 P.3d 884 (Haw. 2008), *rev'd*, 556 U.S. 163 (2009), *vacated as moot*, 219 P.3d 1111 (Haw. 2009).

CHAPTER 1

Kanaka Maoli Genocide

The Native Hawaiians call themselves the Kanaka Maoli. I began working with them at the San Francisco Tribunal in October of 1992. In order to commemorate the 500th anniversary of Columbus's invasion of the Americas, in early 1992 I was asked by the Organizers of the International Tribunal of Indigenous Peoples and Oppressed Nations in the United States to serve as Special Prosecutor of the U.S. Federal government for committing international crimes against indigenous peoples, people of color, and oppressed nationalities living under the control of the United States government. The Tribunal was initiated by the American Indian Movement (A.I.M.) with the support of representatives of the Puerto Rican People, the African American People, the Mexican American People, and "progressive White North Americans." I do not consider myself to be "White" but Green. I am a dual-national Irish and American citizen. During the past 850 years of resisting one of the most brutal and cruel colonial occupations in the history of humankind, we Irish know what the denial of self-determination, gross violations of our most fundamental human rights, and genocide are all about in our beloved Ireland and abroad—atrocities which still continue today.[1]

In my capacity as Special Prosecutor of the United States Federal government, I drew up an Indictment under international law that was served upon the Attorney General of the United States and the United States Attorney in San Francisco prior to the convening of the Tribunal in that city just before "Columbus Day" on October 2-4, 1992 with a demand that they appear to defend the United States government from the charges. I take it they saw no point in trying to defend the indefensible because no one showed up to defend the United States government, though they did publicly acknowledge receipt of our service of process. I will not go through all 37 charges of my Indictment here. But the proceedings of this path-breaking International Tribunal have been recorded in a formal Verdict by the Tribunal; in a Video of the Tribunal; and in a Book on the Tribunal—all under the title *U.S.A. On Trial: The International Tribunal on Indigenous Peoples and Oppressed Nations in the United States.*[2]

Six months after the conclusion of these San Francisco Tribunal proceedings, I was the Lawyer and Ambassador for the Republic of Bosnia and Herzegovina arguing its case for genocide against Yugoslavia before the International Court of Justice in The Hague, the World Court of the United Nations system. There on 8 April 1993 and 13 September 1993, I would singlehandedly win two World Court Orders overwhelmingly in favor of Bosnia against Yugoslavia to cease and desist from committing all acts of genocide against the Bosnians.[3] I treated the San Francisco Tribunal proceedings with as much care, attention, dignity, respect, and professionalism as I did the World Court proceedings for Bosnia. And the results were the same: massive, overwhelming, crushing victories for my clients at both the World Court and the San Francisco Tribunal!

Prior to the opening of the San Francisco proceedings, I met with my client and later friend Dr. Kekuni Blaisdell, M.D., and his *Ohana* (extended family) who had traveled there in order to present the Kanaka Maoli case for genocide against the United States government. I agreed to represent them and to argue their claims. What follows are edited passages from my *Opening Statement* and my *Closing Statement* before the San Francisco, Tribunal on behalf of the Kanaka Maoli and the other indigenous peoples.[4] Many of these same arguments would apply to Canada *pari passu* for its numerous and egregious crimes against indigenous peoples.

Opening Statement
Lead Prosecutor
Francis A. Boyle

Francis A. Boyle: Ladies and gentleman, distinguished Members of the Tribunal. May it please the Tribunal. My name is Francis Boyle, Professor of International Law at the University of Illinois in Champaign. I appear here today on behalf of the indigenous people of the U.S., on behalf of the New Afrikan people, on behalf of the Mexican people, and on behalf of the Puerto Rican people who are the plaintiffs in this proceeding against the federal government of the United States of America, the defendant, for the commission of international crimes, under well recognized principles of international law going back to its foundation in 1787 and continuing until this very moment.

We will establish that the Federal government is an international criminal conspiracy and a criminal organization, just like the Nazi government of World War II Germany. As far as the plaintiffs are concerned there is no difference whatsoever. Indeed, we will prove our case by using the precise same law that the United States government itself applied to the defeated Nazi war criminals at the Nuremburg Tribunal in 1945. Speaking at that time, Mr. Justice Robert Jackson who was on leave from the United States Supreme Court to serve as Chief Prosecutor at Nuremburg said, and I only paraphrase, that the standard of law that the United States government was imposing at Nuremburg would be a universal standard of law, there would not be two standards – one for the victor and one for the vanquished. But rather, that it would only be fair to hold the U.S. government fully accountable by the same standards that were applied by Nuremburg. Today, 47 years later, we are going to take Mr. Justice Jackson at his word and hold the federal government of the United States fully accountable for international crimes against indigenous peoples and people of color throughout its two hundred year history. You have already received a copy of the indictment that I was instructed to draw up by the plaintiffs I represent.

Let me briefly address the question of jurisdiction, your right to consider the charges against the defendant. In the Judgment of the Nuremburg Tribunal and also the Judgment of the Tokyo War Crimes Tribunal of 1945 against defeated Japanese war criminals, it was made quite clear that all citizens of the world community have both the right and the duty under international law, to sit in judgment on a gross and consistent pattern of violations of international criminal law committed by any member state of the world community. Furthermore, article 38 paragraph one, sub-paragraph D of the World Court Statute, provides that judicial decisions are a subsidiary means for the determination of the rules of international law. You will be called upon to render a judicial decision within the meaning of the Statute of the International Court of Justice. The decision that you render will be on par in terms of judicial precedence and significance with the judicial decision rendered by any other international tribunal or the Supreme Court of the countries from which you come. So understand, this is not a mock trial—this is not a mock tribunal. We are here to do a judicial job that has been charged to us by international law and we will create legal precedent. In whatever you decide to do.

Now, in this indictment you have 37 charges against the federal government of the United States of America on behalf of the four groups of peoples who are here as plaintiffs. You have read through these charges and the members of the audience have read through them. I will not go through them one at a time, but I will set out the basic thrust of our legal case under international law. The particulars of this case will then be detailed by the special prosecutors who represent each one of the four groups who are appearing today as plaintiffs.

The heart of the indictment goes back to the Nuremburg Charter of 1945 which the U.S. government itself used to prosecute defeated Nazi war criminals and later the same body of law to prosecute defeated Japanese war criminals. We have alleged that the United States government has committed Nuremburg crimes against indigenous people and people of color in North America: Crimes against Peace. Planning, preparation, initiation, waging a war of aggression or a war in violation international treaties, agreements, or assurances. Or participation in a common plan or conspiracy for the accomplishment of these purposes. Here in particular, the Puerto Rican people, the Mexican people, the Native American peoples all have very strong claims, that you will hear, that they have been the victim of numerous Nuremburg Crimes against Peace.

Nuremburg War Crimes are defined as the violations of the laws and customs of war: murder, ill-treatment, deportation to slave labor, or any other maltreatment of the civilian population. Murder or ill-treatment of prisoners of war or persons on the seas, killing of hostages. Plunder of public and private property. Wanton destruction of cities, towns, or villages. Devastation not justified by military necessity. You will hear evidence that all four groups of plaintiffs have been subjected to these practices.

Finally, Crimes against Humanity. And here, let me recall that the notion of Crime against Humanity was put into the Nuremburg Charter to deal with Hitler's attempt to exterminate the Jewish people. In our opinion, the defendant has perpetrated the exact same offense against Native peoples, African people, Puerto Rican people, and the Mexican people here in the United States. There is no legal difference. It is guilty of Crimes against Humanity. And let me quote you this definition of a Crime against Humanity: "Murder, extermination, enslavement, deportation, and other inhumane acts committed against any civilian population or persecutions on political, racial, or religious grounds, etc."

Now one point that might concern you is the fact that the Nuremburg Charter was promulgated in 1945. How can we use this law to examine practices by the U.S. government going back to 1787?[5] First, it is our position that these offenses are still continuing today, against Native peoples and people of color, here in North America. These are ongoing offenses that have a long history – in some cases going back 500 years. This needs to be dealt with by the Tribunal. Second, when it came to the promulgation of the Nuremburg Charter, the U.S. government had no problem with signing a treaty in 1945, and applying it to behavior that had been committed by the Nazi government from the time of its foundation in 1933, up to and including, 1945. Well, what is sauce for the goose, is sauce for the gander.

There is no statute of limitations under international law for the commission of international crimes. We are simply going to hold the U.S. government accountable under these same standards, but instead of going back to 1933, we will go back to 1787. But I want to make it clear, our position is that these crimes are continuing today. Now, a crime against humanity was later codified in the Genocide Convention of 1948 that the U.S. government is a party to. Again, remember the paradigmatic example is what Hitler did to the Jews, and we believe it is the same thing that the federal government has done to Native peoples, Mexicans, African people, *Kanaka Maoli* (indigenous Hawaiians) and the Puerto Rican people.

I will read for you the legal test for genocide from the Genocide Convention that codifies the concept of Crime against Humanity. Genocide means any of the following acts committed with intent to destroy, in whole or in part—we do not have to prove that the federal government has succeeded in destroying completely any one individual group of people, although there is evidence that it has completely destroyed several groups of Native American people. Intent to destroy in whole or in part a national, ethnic, racial, or religious group as such—and either one of those characteristics would qualify. In our opinion, all four groups fall into one or more of those categories, national, ethnic, racial, or religious. Some of them meet all four qualifications, and certainly the Native American people doing it. So the following acts are genocide: Killing members of the group, causing serious bodily harm, or mental harm to members of the group. This opens up the psychological trauma that these people have been subjected to for the past 205 years. Deliberately inflicting on the group conditions of life calculated to bring about its physical destruction in whole or in part.

All indigenous people and people of color living under the imperial domain of the federal government fit within that definition of genocide. Every one of them. The federal government is inflicting today, and historically has deliberately inflicted on all of them conditions of life calculated to bring about their physical destruction in whole or in part. Imposing measures intended to prevent births within the group. You will see a pattern of the federal government historically undertaking policies to prevent births of Native peoples, peoples of color, subject to their control, including wide-scale sterilization of Native peoples and peoples of color. And finally, forcibly transferring children of the group to another group. Again, you will receive evidence of that reprehensible behavior.

Now, in the indictment we have also alleged numerous violations of human rights treaties. You have those in the indictment. I will not bother to repeat all of it except to point out that the special prosecutors will develop a gross and consistent pattern of violations of fundamental human rights against indigenous people and people of color by the United States government for the past 205 years.

The basic source for these human rights is the Universal Declaration of Human Rights of 1948, which you have already looked at. The U.S. government considers the Universal Declaration of Human Rights to be binding, as a matter of customary international law. We intend to take the United States at its word. Compare its behavior with the provisions of this document, and you will see that the United States government has violated each and every one of these provisions when it comes to indigenous people and people of color subject to its control. The Universal Declaration was then codified in two United Nations human rights covenants in 1966. The International Covenant on Civil and Political Rights and the International Covenant on Economic, Social and Cultural Rights. The United States government has recently ratified the International Covenant on Civil and Political rights. So again, it is only fair for you to evaluate their behavior under that treaty. The Economic, Social, and Cultural Convention has not yet been ratified by the United States government, but it has been signed. Under the Vienna Convention on the Law of Treaties, the U.S. government is obligated to act in a manner so as not to defeat the object and purpose of the Economic, Social, and Cultural Convention until it has given an indication whether or not it will ratify. Again, it is fair to compare its behavior under this treaty and you will find it severely lacking, not only for indigenous people and people of color in America, but for all people in North America.

The indictment also refers to the Racial Discrimination Convention, we all know what racial discrimination is about. Our position is that the U.S. government is the paradigmatic example of a racist state in international relations today. It is even worse than South Africa.

Indeed, the United States of America is the grossest violator of human rights of any state in the world today. Although this is not subject to your jurisdiction, look at the quarter of a million people that the U.S. government exterminated in Iraq, in 100 days. If you allow the U.S. government to get away with it, this is what they are going to do to indigenous people and people of color here on the North American continent. Iraq is the future, unless you do something about it.

I also refer to the Apartheid Convention. The U.S.

government has signed but again, not yet ratified the Racial Discrimination Convention so it is bound generally to adhere to its terms to the Racial Discrimination Convention. It has not signed the Convention Against Apartheid. Why? Because the U.S. government practices a system of Apartheid against people of color and indigenous people here in the United States, just as reprehensible and heinous as what the South African government has done to its Black people in South Africa. That is why it has refused to sign the Apartheid Convention, but that should not deter you because this is a reflection of the Nuremburg concept of Crime against Humanity, which the U.S. is bound to. Apartheid is defined as a variant of Crime against Humanity. I submit that you can only conclude that the United States practices apartheid, as defined by this Convention, against indigenous people and people of color in North America.

....

The final count of the indictment states that the U.S. government is an international criminal conspiracy and a criminal organization in accordance with the Nuremburg Charter, Judgment, and Principles. This is exactly what happened at Nuremburg, where the Judgment determined, the Tribunal determined that various organs of the Nazi state were criminal organizations and that mere membership in any of these organizations, such as the S.S., the Gestapo, etc., was a criminal act.

Again, our position is the federal government of the United States is legally identical to the Nazi government. Indeed, the crimes of the Nazi government were so enormous under international criminal law that it was dissolved as a legal and political entity. It no longer exists today. The current government of Germany, the Federal Republic of Germany is not a successor in law to the Nazi government. It no longer exists. We are asking you to do the exact same thing to the United States federal government. We are asking you to issue an order determining that the United States federal government is an international criminal conspiracy and a criminal organization. We are asking you to issue an order dissolving the United States federal government as a legal and political entity. Just as happened to the Nazi government.

And finally, we are asking you to recognize that the sovereignty —international legal sovereignty over the lands inhabited by Native peoples, Mexicans, the New African Black people, and the Puerto Rican people resides in the hands of the people themselves and not in the hands of the federal government, which is a criminal organization. Again, this is pursuant to their right of self determination under international law. We believe that a judgment by this Tribunal along these lines will then prepare the way for these peoples to apply for membership as independent states in the United Nations organization.

Just recently, the world witnessed the collapse of the Soviet Union, an empire in its own right. Lenin had once called the Czarist empire "the slave house of nationalities." Well, we have another slave house of nationalities and that is the United States of America federal government. We are asking you to dissolve this enormous slave house of nationalities, that has repressed, terrorized, intimidated, and exterminated indigenous people and people of color in North America. As the Soviet Union, an empire, collapsed and freed these peoples, so too the American empire must collapse as well. The collapse of the American empire is the only way to save the existence of indigenous people and people of color living subject to its control. It is up to you to produce that result. The beginning of the end of the American empire starts here and today and is in your hands. Thank you.

....

Closing Statements
Lead Prosecutor
Francis A. Boyle

....

Francis Boyle: Distinguished members of this Tribunal: Ladies and Gentlemen, may it please the Tribunal. This morning I told you that we would put on evidence today that would prove that the Federal government of the United States is an international criminal conspiracy organization that is legally and factually identical to the Nazi government of Adolph Hitler when it comes to the treatment of indigenous peoples and people of color in North America and around the world. And I submit to you that that is exactly what we have done in the oral testimony that you have heard today and also in the extensive written documentation that has been submitted to you and that you will be able to examine tomorrow during the course of your deliberations.

Now obviously, I will not be able to review all of this mass of evidence that covers 205 years and ultimately goes back 500 years, but I wanted to highlight a few salient facts for your consideration that you must keep in mind during your deliberations that are crucial for the future of indigenous peoples and people of color, subject to the control of the United States government. My clients from Hawaii have pointed out that they were a victim of a Nuremburg Crime against Peace by the invasion of the United States government against the sovereign, independent Kingdom of Hawaii. During the course of this invasion and after this invasion they were subjected to numerous war crimes and Crimes against Humanity, as defined by the Nuremburg Charter. And let me return again to the textbook definition of "crime against humanity": murder, extermination, enslavement, deportation, and other inhumane acts committed against any civilian population or persecutions on political or racial or religious grounds. We have been able to establish all of that.

Indeed, we had testimony here today that only 6,000 pure indigenous people live in Hawaii, and that it is projected by that the year 2040, they will be extinguished. Now let me make it clear to you then: that this is precisely the reason why you must give me the order dissolving the Federal Government of the United States of America.[6]

If you do not give me that order, the Hawaiian people will be exterminated, extinguished, just like Hitler tried, but failed to do, to the Jewish people. Are you going to let the United States government get away with it?

We have heard testimony on genocide with respect to all indigenous peoples and people of color, here, subject to the control of the United States. And let me repeat the actions which comprise the definition of genocide: killing members of the group; causing serious bodily or mental harm to members of the group; deliberately inflicting on the group conditions of life calculated to bring about its physical destruction, in whole or in part; imposing measures intended to prevent births within the group; and forcibly transferring children of the group to another group.

We have heard evidence that all these acts of genocide have been committed in one fashion or another against the Native American people, African American people, the Mexican American people, and the Puerto Rican people. We have heard about Indian children being taken away from their homes and their families and subjected to enormous fatality rates in so-called boarding schools where they died by themselves, without their families.

We have heard mention of the doctrine of Manifest Destiny, upon which the defendant, the Federal government, is supposed to have been founded. Well, let me point out that this doctrine sounds and looks like, indeed, preceded Hitler's doctrine of *Lebensraum* ("Living Space"). Only Hitler decided to move to the East. The Federal government of the United States decided to move to the West, but the results were exactly the same thing: millions upon millions of people were killed because they were deemed to be inferior races.

There is no legal or factual distinction except that the United States government of America killed tens of millions more than Hitler and Nazi regime were ever able to do. And we heard a figure that approximately 100 million Africans were killed during the slave trade or as a result of the slave trade.

We have all heard that Hitler killed 6 million Jews, 20 million Russians, 2 million Poles, 500,000 Gypsies, but how often have we heard that the slave trade here that went on under the control of the United States federal government, killed 100 million Africans?

We have heard testimony that slavery is the absolute negation of human rights; human beings treated as chattel. We have heard that the federal government of the United States of America, in the Thirteenth Amendment, was supposed to have freed the slaves, and yet what really happened was that it turned the slaves into serfs. Let me compare this to what happened in Czarist Russia, that slave house of nationalities, as Lenin called it. At the same time, in 1861, the Great Liberator Czar, Alexander II, turned the serfs into free people. And in America, they were kept serfs legally, for at least another 100 years. This is the dimension of the historical problem that you are dealing with; that you have to come to grips with.

The United States federal government today is the modern slave house of nationalities for indigenous peoples and people of color, and it is up to you to set them free by dissolving the federal government of the United States of America. This is the only remedy that can stop these Crimes against Humanity, war crimes, further Crimes against Peace, especially against indigenous peoples.

....I have received a question from Judge Fausett raising the issue of what we lawyers call the intertemporal rule, that is, how do we take standards of international law that have been developed from 1945, and apply them to examine a history going back 500 years and in the case of the United States government, back to 1787?[7]

The first point to keep in mind is that there is a history of 500 years of continuing violations of known standards of law, even as they existed at that time, up until today. This is not history; this is the present, and it will be the future, for indigenous peoples and people of color, unless you act today.

Second, it was well recognized, even at the time when these offenses were being perpetrated by the Federal government and its predecessors at law, the British colonial occupying forces, that there were such things as common law crimes: murder, rape, robbery, arson, kidnapping, mayhem, larceny, theft. All of these things were well known to be crimes, subject to the death penalty, when they were committed by white people upon white people. That was the common punishment at common law: death for committing any of these common law felonies. And yet, when these exact same crimes were perpetrated upon indigenous peoples and people of color, there was no penalty whatsoever attached, because they were viewed to be less than human: to be property. White settlers could do what they wanted to do with them. But the legal principle was still the same. They knew when they did what they did that it was criminal activity, under common law principles.

So it is completely fair today to hold the United States government fully accountable for a long history of 205 years of organized criminal activity against indigenous peoples and people of color. And it's not terribly important what you call it. Call it a Crime against Humanity. Call it genocide. Call it murder. Call it slavery, kidnapping. I don't care. But it is clearly criminal.

It is clearly organized. It is clearly a conspiracy. And the United States government is clearly a criminal organization.

....

This gets us then, into the broader questions raised in the testimony by the representatives of the New Afrikan people. We have a situation in the United States today, in which the white power structure which runs this country knows that people of color will become a majority in this country sometime between the year 2020 and 2030. They know that. They are afraid of it. And they are doing everything they can do to stop it. And understand that this is organized, systematic governmental policy. We have seen evidence of it here today: the incarceration rate for people of color and indigenous peoples; executions; murder; the war on drugs; health care; education; everything purposely designed to reduce the number of people of color and indigenous peoples in North America, to prevent them from becoming a majority here, in the United States of America. And that is the dilemma; that is the problem faced by people of color and indigenous peoples in the United States today. A government setting out purposely and maliciously to extinguish some of them, especially the indigenous peoples, and to reduce and to limit the numbers of all the rest of them. It is up to you, the members of this Tribunal, to stop the federal government, the C.I.A., the military-industrial complex, the white power structure that runs this country.

I have asked you for four types of relief toward that end: First, guilty as charged on all 37 counts of this indictment. Second, an order proscribing the United States federal government as an international criminal conspiracy and a criminal organization, just as was done to the Nazi government. Third, an order dissolving the federal government of the United States of America as a legal and political entity, once again, just as was done to the Nazi government.

Fourth, and finally, I ask that recognition by this Tribunal be made, that the sovereignty over the lands inhabited by indigenous peoples and peoples of color, that is, the Native American peoples, the New African people, the Mexicano people, the Puerto Rican people; that legal sovereignty has always resided, today resides, and will continue to reside in the hands of these peoples themselves.

> Distinguished members of this Tribunal, make no mistake about it, the future of indigenous peoples and people of color in North America, depend upon you giving this judgment with those four forms of relief. Thank you.

The distinguished Judges composing this International Tribunal consisted of seven independent Experts on human rights drawn from all over the world. In their Verdict, Preliminary Findings, and Order of 4 October 1992, the Indigenous Peoples' Tribunal did not accept all of the 37 charges that I filed in my Indictment against the United States government for perpetrating international crimes against indigenous peoples, people of color, and oppressed nations. But most strikingly, when it came to the Kanaka Maoli, the International Tribunal accepted my charge of genocide against the United States government, and by a unanimous vote at that. In its own words, the exact ruling of the San Francisco Tribunal on behalf of the Kanaka Maoli was as follows:

> **HAWAIIAN PEOPLES**
>
> 6. The Tribunal further accepts a motion by the Prosecutor for the Native American Peoples to amend the face of the Indictment to include the following allegation, which the Tribunal unanimously finds has been sufficiently proved by the evidence it has received:
>
> > **The Federal Government of the United States of America has perpetrated crimes of genocide against the Kanaka Maoli (the Indigenous Hawaiian People) and has engaged in actions constituting gross violations of their human rights and their right to self-determination, all of which threaten to render the Kanaka Maoli extinct.**

As Special Prosecutor for the Tribunal, it came as no surprise to me that the Judges unanimously accepted all of my charges of genocide against the United States government with respect to the Kanaka Maoli and Hawaii. This is because the principles of international law with respect to the Kanaka Maoli and Hawaii are incontestable, and thus so glaringly obvious for the entire world to see. I most respectfully submit that the Kanaka Maoli and their supporters must use this ruling and the San Francisco Tribunal's Verdict, Preliminary Findings, and Order with a view to supporting, promoting, and defending their basic rights under international law going forward, including their right to self-determination and to re-establish the independent Kanaka Maoli Nation State of Hawaii. In the final section of its Verdict, the San Francisco Tribunal also rendered the following unanimous decision that directly concerns the international legal rights of the Kanaka Maoli and Hawaii:

> **ADDITIONAL FINDINGS**
>
> In light of the foregoing findings, this Tribunal also, by unanimous vote, finds the Defendant guilty as charged in paragraph 37, which, as amended, reads:
>
>> **In light of the foregoing international crimes, the Defendant constitutes a Criminal Conspiracy and a Criminal Organization in accordance with the Nuremberg Charter, Judgment, and Principles and the other sources of public international law specified above, and the Federal Government of the United States of America is similar to the Nazi government of World War II Germany.**

This powerful Finding speaks for itself and requires no explanation by me.

The Tribunal concluded its Verdict with the following Order to the United States government: "Now therefore, it is ordered, adjudged and decreed that the Defendant cease and desist from the commission of the crimes it has been found guilty of herein." Pursuant thereto, I then filed a copy of this San Francisco Verdict with its Cease and Desist Order upon the Attorney General of the United States of America in Washington, D.C.

In return, I later received a 5 February 1993 Letter from the U.S. Department of Justice that acknowledged the receipt of the San Francisco Tribunal Verdict and its Cease and Desist Order against the United States government. This U.S. D.O.J Letter then advised me: "If you, or the Tribunal, have any evidence of the violation of federal criminal law, we ask that you provide that information to your local office of the Federal Bureau of Investigation."

As I saw it at the time, and still see it as of today, historically this would be analogous to the Nazi Ministry of "Justice" advising a German lawyer representing the Jews to file his Complaint of criminal law violations by the Nazi government against the Jews with the Gestapo.

The F.B.I. is and has always been the American Gestapo[8]—especially for all indigenous peoples and peoples of color living within its imperial domain including the Kanaka Maoli.

The Verdict, Preliminary Findings, and Order of this San Francisco Tribunal qualify as a "judicial decision" within the meaning of Article 38(1)(d) of the Statute of the International Court of Justice. What this means is that this Verdict, Preliminary Findings, and Order constitute "subsidiary means for the determination of rules of law" for international law and practice. They contribute to the general international understanding of what factors are entailed and must be addressed in the context of applying international law to situations such as that of the Kanaka Maoli and other indigenous peoples. So the activity of holding such a Tribunal contributes to pushing the global understanding forward, not just as it relates to the Kanaka Maoli, but also as it concerns other indigenous peoples and victims of colonialism, aggression, genocide, and self-determination, how these impact other peoples worldwide, and how they should be viewed and resolved. This is so because the Statute of the International Court of Justice is an "integral part" of the United Nations Charter under Article 92 thereof.

Hence the San Francisco Tribunal's Verdict, Preliminary Findings, and Order can be relied upon by the International Court of Justice itself, by the International Criminal Court, by some other International Tribunal, or by any other Court in the world today, as well as by any People or State of the World Community—including and especially by the Kanaka Maoli and their supporters—in order to prosecute their claims for genocide, self-determination, and independence.

The Verdict of the San Francisco Tribunal also serves as adequate notice to the appropriate officials in the United States Federal government that they bear personal criminal responsibility under international law and the domestic legal systems of all Peoples and States in the World Community for implementing and perpetrating these illegal, criminal and reprehensible policies and practices against indigenous peoples and peoples of color living in North America, and especially against the Kanaka Maoli and Hawaii.

The 1992 San Francisco Tribunal marked the start of my efforts to **restore the Kingdom of Hawaii!**

ENDNOTES

1 Francis A. Boyle, United Ireland, Human Rights, and International Law (2012).

2 American Indian Movement, Verdict of the International Tribunal of Indigenous Peoples and Oppressed Nations in the USA (San Francisco, CA: Oct. 4, 1992); Puerto Rican Cultural Center, USA on Trial: The International Tribunal on Indigenous Peoples and Oppressed Nations in the United States (Chicago, IL: 1996); Mission Creek Video, USA on Trial (Parts I & II): The International Tribunal of Indigenous Peoples and Oppressed Nations in the USA (San Francisco, CA 941141-1271). A free download of this video can be found on the internet at: http://www.archive.org/details/ddtv_131_usa_on_trial.

3 Francis A. Boyle, The Bosnian People Charge Genocide (1996).

4 *See* Puerto Rican Cultural Center, USA on Trial, *supra* note 2, at 23-36, 263-67, 269-71, 273-75.

5 The date of the United States Constitution.

6 INDICTMENT OF THE FEDERAL GOVERNMENT OF THE UNITED STATES OF AMERICA FOR THE COMMISSION OF INTERNATIONAL CRIMES AND PETITION FOR ORDERS MANDATING ITS PROSCRIPTION AND DISSOLUTION AS AN INTERNATIONAL CRIMINAL CONSPIRACY AND A CRIMINAL ORGANIZATION

Introduction

All citizens of the World Community have both the right and the duty under public international law to sit in judgment over a gross and consistent pattern of violations of the most fundamental norms of international criminal law committed by any member state of that same World Community.

Such is the case for the International Tribunal of Indigenous Peoples and Oppressed Nationalities in the United States of America that convenes in San Francisco during the weekend of October 1-4, 1992. Its weighty but important task is to examine the long history of international criminal activity that has been perpetrated by the Federal Government of the United States of America against the Indigenous Peoples and Peoples of Color living in North America since it was founded in 1787.

Toward that end, I have the honor to present to the Members of this Tribunal the following charges against the Federal Government of the United States of America under international criminal law. In light of the gravity, severity, and longstanding nature of these international crimes and also in light of the fact that the Federal Government of the United States of America appears to be irrevocably committed to continuing down this path of lawlessness and criminality against Indigenous Peoples and Peoples of Color living in North America and elsewhere, I hereby petition the Members of this Tribunal to issue an Order proscribing the Federal Government of the United States of America as an International Criminal Conspiracy and a Criminal Organization under the Nuremberg Charter, Judgment, and Principles as well as the other sources of public international law specified below. For that reason, I also request that the Members of this Tribunal issue an Order dissolving the Federal Government of the United States of America as a legal and political entity. Finally, I ask this Tribunal to declare that international legal sovereignty over the Territories principally inhabited by the Native American Peoples, the New Afrikan People, the Mexicano People, and the People of Puerto Rico resides in the hands of these respective Peoples Themselves.

....

An International Criminal Conspiracy and a Criminal Organization

37. In light of the foregoing international crimes, the Defendant constitutes an International Criminal Conspiracy and a Criminal Organization in accordance with the Nuremberg Charter, Judgment, and Principles and the other sources of public international law specified above. The Federal Government of the United States of America is legally identical to the Nazi government of World War II Germany. Indeed, the Defendant's President, George Bush, has proclaimed a so-called New World Order that sounds and looks strikingly similar to the New Order proclaimed by Adolph Hitler over fifty years ago.

Conclusion

Like unto a pirate, the Defendant is *hostis humani generis*: The enemy of all humankind! For the good of all humanity, this Tribunal must condemn and repudiate the Federal Government of the United States of America and its grotesque vision of a New World Order that is constructed upon warfare, bloodshed, violence, criminality, genocide, racism, colonialism, apartheid, massive violations of fundamental human rights, and the denial of the international legal right of self-determination to the Indigenous Peoples and Peoples of Color living in North America and elsewhere around the world.

Consequently, this Tribunal must find the Defendant guilty as charged on all of the counts specified above beyond a reasonable doubt. This Tribunal must also issue an Order that formally proscribes the Federal Government of the United States of America as an International Criminal Conspiracy and a Criminal Organization. This Tribunal must also issue a separate Order mandating the dissolution of the Federal Government of the United States of America as a legal and political entity. Finally, this Tribunal must declare that international legal sovereignty over the Territories principally inhabited by the Native American Peoples, the New Afrikan People, the Mexicano People, and the People of Puerto Rico resides, respectively, in the hands of these Peoples Themselves. The very lives, well-being, health, welfare, and safety of the Indigenous Peoples and Peoples of Color living in North America and elsewhere around the world depend upon the ultimate success of your deliberations.

Respectfully submitted by,

FRANCIS A. BOYLE
PROFESSOR OF INTERNATIONAL LAW
SPECIAL PROSECUTOR

Dated: September 18, 1992

7 The date of the United States Constitution.

8 *See* M. Wesley Swearingen, FBI Secrets: An Agent's Exposé (1995).

CHAPTER 2

KANAKA MAOLI SOVEREIGNTY

Sometime during the early Fall of 1993, I received a telephone call from Mr. Pu'uhonua ["Bumpy"] Kanahele who identified himself as a Native Hawaiian, the leader of the Ohana Council, and a Commissioner of the Hawaiian Sovereignty Advisory Commission (HSAC) for the State of Hawaii. Mr. Kanahele informed me that he and his people were giving serious consideration to moving toward independence. In his capacity as HSAC Commissioner, Mr. Kanahele invited me to come out to Hawaii and speak before the HSAC and to Kanaka Maoli leaders about the international legal right of the Native Hawaiian People to establish an independent nation state of their own. I informed Mr. Kanahele that I would be happy to do this, but that outstanding professional commitments for Bosnia at the World Court would prevent me from coming to Hawaii until the end of December 1993.

Mr. Kanahele then put me in touch with Ms. Lulani McKenzie, who was the Executive Director of HSAC. All three of us agreed that I would travel out to Hawaii during the last week of December 1993. We further agreed that I would give one public lecture to the HSAC Commissioners and the general public on the right of the Native Hawaiian People to establish an independent state of their own, and specifically with reference to Public Law No. 103-150, the so-called Apology Resolution. (The official text of the Apology Resolution is set forth below at the end of this chapter.) We also agreed that I would make one personal appearance before the HSAC Commissioners to answer any questions they might have about my public lecture. In return, Ms. McKenzie informed me that the State of Hawaii would pay all of my out-of-pocket expenses incident to my trip to Hawaii and a modest Honorarium for my professional services. These terms were acceptable to me. The State of Hawaii did indeed pay all of my out-of-pocket expenses and I was later sent a check by the State of Hawaii signed by then Governor Waihee, a Kanaka Maoli himself, for the Honorarium. Therefore, I considered myself to have been hired by the State of Hawaii as an official consultant on international law to HSAC and to the Commissioners, including Mr. Kanahele, for the aforementioned purposes.

On Sunday, December 26, 1993, I flew to Hawaii and met Mr. Kanahele and his advisers for the first time. He immediately proceeded to seek my legal advice and counsel as to the establishment of an independent nation state for Native Hawaiians. Therefore, I date the establishment of my attorney-client relationship with Mr. Kanahele and the Ohana Council to these conversations on December 26, 1993. These conversations with Mr. Kanahele continued almost fulltime until my departure from Hawaii on the late evening of Thursday, December 30, 1993.

On the evening of December 28, 1993, I gave a public lecture to the general public and the Hawaiian Sovereignty Advisory Commission on the subject of "The Restoration of the Independent Nation State of Hawaii Under International Law" at Mable Smyth Hall in Honolulu under the official auspices of HSAC. My Address and the question-and-answer session with the Commissioners and the members of the public took approximately three hours. Mr. Kanahele sat in the audience with the other HSAC Commissioners for the entire Address and question-and-answer session.

The very next morning, on December 29, 1993, I made a personal appearance before the HSAC Commissioners at a government building in downtown Honolulu to answer any questions they might have about my Address the preceding evening. This session was open to the public, but essentially it was designed to permit a dialogue between the Commissioners and me. This session lasted approximately three hours. Mr. Kanahele was present at this session for the entire time in his capacity as HSAC Commissioner.

Later that day, and after further consultations with me, Mr. Kanahele decided to resign as HSAC Commissioner because he concluded that his fellow Commissioners were not seriously interested in considering the option of creating an independent nation state for Native Hawaiians. Sometime after my departure from Hawaii on 30 December 1993, Mr. Kanahele informed Governor Waihee of his decision to resign from HSAC for these reasons.

While I was still in Hawaii, however, Mr. Kanahele asked me to help draft the functional equivalent of a Declaration of Independence for him, the Ohana Council, and all Native Hawaiian People. I agreed to do this free of charge. This document was completed just before my departure from Hawaii. Pursuant to conversations I had with Mr. Kanahele, we decided to call this document "Proclamation Restoring the Independence of the Sovereign Nation State of Hawaii." The official English language translation of this Proclamation can be found in the next chapter below. The authentic version is in Hawaiian.

During my time in Hawaii, and at my express request, Mr. Kanahele took me around the Hawaiian Islands to meet his people at their homes and encampments on the beaches of Hawaii. During these meetings, I gave many lectures that basically repeated the substance of my 28 December 1993 Address, and answered any questions these Native Hawaiians might have. I estimate that I gave approximately two to three lectures per day for every day I was in Hawaii. Mr. Kanahele attended almost all of these lectures in his then current capacity as HSAC Commissioner.

Certainly the most eloquent, poignant and concise question I received during my 1993 lecture tour of Hawaii was from an elderly Kupuna living at a beach encampment on the Big Island of Hawaii while speaking under a picnic shelter: "Professor Boyle, why are you the first person to come out here and tell us what our rights are?" I had no answer to her question. But I was greatly happy to be there. On a purely personal level, that Auntie Kupuna and her question made my entire trip to Hawaii worthwhile.

Quite frankly, as a human being and as a lawyer, I was appalled by the atrocious conditions in which these Native Hawaiians were forced to live in a beautiful land that was once all their own. I flew back home on the late evening of Thursday, December 30, 1993 in order to arrive on time to spend New Year's Eve with my wife. I have remained in continuous contact with Mr. Kanahele and his people by phone, fax, mail, and email since then.

On 16 January 1994, Mr. Kanahele, the Ohana Council, and a fairly large number of Native Hawaiians declared their independence from the United States for all Native Hawaiians and issued the Proclamation to that effect that I helped them draft at the Iolani Palace. Soon thereafter, Mr. Kanahele and his people established themselves as the Independent Nation State of Hawaii. Mr. Kanahele asked me to serve as Legal Adviser to the Nation of Hawaii, which I agreed to do. Thereafter, I have provided legal advice and counsel to Mr. Kanahele and the citizens of the Nation of Hawaii concerning the establishment of their state continuously until today. I have also given them legal advice and counsel concerning the protection of the basic human rights of all Native Hawaiians continuously until today. I have also given advice, counsel and representation to several other Kanaka Maoli leaders and organizations.

Pursuant to Mr. Kanahele's request, I participated in drafting a Constitution for the Nation of Hawaii free of charge. The official text can be found in chapter three of this book. Upon the adoption of the Constitution by the citizens of the Nation of Hawaii, Mr. Kanahele became Head of State of the Nation of Hawaii. In this capacity, Mr. Kanahele was entitled to receive all the privileges and immunities, respect and deference, that must be accorded to a Head of State as required by the general principles of public international law. During my many conversations with Mr. Kanahele over the phone and in person he has repeatedly emphasized to me the critical importance of adopting exclusively peaceful and nonviolent means for the establishment of the Nation of Hawaii in accordance with the Native Hawaiian Spirit of Aloha. I have never had any reason to doubt Mr. Kanahele's sincere commitment to the pursuit of peaceful, nonviolent means for the establishment of the Nation of Hawaii in the Spirit of Aloha. It is the Kanaka Maoli Spirit of Aloha that will ***Free Hawaii!***

Here is the edited speech that I delivered on that occasion.

RESTORATION OF THE INDEPENDENT NATION STATE OF HAWAII UNDER INTERNATIONAL LAW

Professor Francis Anthony Boyle
Mable Smyth Hall, Honolulu, Oahu, Hawaii
December 28, 1993

I'm very happy to be here this evening with you, and I'm very honored that the Sovereignty Commission would invite me to come and speak this evening. I also want to express my gratitude to Bumpy Kanahele and the members of the Ohana Council who have been serving as my sponsors for the week that I'm here.

Now as I understand it the Sovereignty Commission[1] is looking into models, examples, of where the native people of Hawaii can go in light of the state legislation that has been adopted and also now in light of the recent federal statute, the Overthrow of Hawaii Resolution (Public Law 103-150),[2] effectively a U.S. apology for having invaded Hawaii, that has just been signed into law by President Clinton [see Appendix below]. I've been asked to come here tonight to discuss one particular model for the future for Native Hawaiian people to consider. Understand, I was not invited here to go through all the possibilities that you might have. I'm happy to comment on some of them if you have questions and give you my opinion about them. And understand, it is not for me to tell Native Hawaiian people what to do. You have to decide for yourselves. But one thing I can do is to describe a particular vision of the future; how you might go about achieving it; what would be the consequences; what would be the basis of authority for doing it—particularly in light of Public Law 103-150[3] signed by President Clinton.

When I read the Public Law for the first time, the first thought that occurred to me is that now the United States government, after one hundred years, has finally and officially conceded, as a matter of United States law, that Native Hawaiian people have the right to restore the independent nation state that you had in 1893 when the United States government came and destroyed it. And also then that as a matter of international law the Native Hawaiian people have the right to go out now and certainly proclaim the restoration of that state. I'm not talking about the State of Hawaii as part of the United States of America. Rather I am talking about an independent state under international law, and ultimately someday a member of the United Nations Organization and other international organizations.

Now here there is a recent example that had been pursued by the Palestinian people who in 1988 decided of their own accord to proclaim their own state,[4] and this was a decision taken by the Palestinian people as a whole. It was subject to a majority vote because there was not unanimous consent, but even those who opposed agreed to be bound by a majority vote. In 1988 they unilaterally proclaimed their own state in a declaration of independence. This unilateral declaration of independence eventually led to the Palestinian state being recognized today by one hundred twenty-five (125) nation states in the world.[5] Now you don't read about that much in the United States because the United States government is one of the few governments in the world to oppose the Palestinian state.

But almost all of Latin America, Africa, and Asia recognize the existence of the state of Palestine. Again, these are indigenous people, like Native Hawaiians, striving for their right of self-determination. And indeed the Palestinians have the requisite votes to be admitted to the United Nations Organization as a sovereign independent nation state, and yet it is the threat of a United States veto that has prevented the admission of the state into the United Nations Organization.[6] But even then this has not prevented the vast majority of the states in the world from recognizing the existence of their state. And even most of Europe would accord them formal de jure diplomatic recognition if not for pressure brought to bear by the United States government. So many of the European states, which are the last holdouts, are today according them de facto recognition as an independent state—that is they are treating them as if they are an independent state without formally coming out and announcing it.

So this is one model to consider that I'll discuss. Not that the plight of the Palestinians is on all fours with Native Hawaiians, but there too you have a situation of massive violations of fundamental human rights and people living under a regime of military occupation. In their case for the last forty-five years, in your case for the last 100 years. So I'll be discussing some of the parallels with that process, and what could be the Native Hawaiian process in the event that you were to decide to move in that direction.

And understand I'm not here to survey all of the possibilities you might have. I'm prepared to comment on them. There are other options you could consider—autonomy; semi-sovereignty; returning to Article 73 status at the United Nations,[7] which states:

> Members of the United Nations which have or assume responsibilities for the administration of territories whose peoples have *not yet* attained a full measure of self-government recognize the principle that the interest of the inhabitants of these territories are

> paramount, and accept as a sacred trust the obligation to promote to the utmost...the well-being of the inhabitants of these territories ... [italics added]

There are various different types of status. But again from my perspective, independence is the route that other people in your situation have chosen to go, and there is ample authority and precedent under international law for the Native Hawaiians to decide to move in that direction.

Now let me start by saying how can this be done, why can you do it? That is, what I am suggesting is that you not ask the permission of the United States Congress to declare independence, but rather you exercise your right of self-determination, that has been afforded to you, the Hawaiian people, by the United Nations Charter, Article 1, paragraph 2: The purposes of the United Nations are...[t]o develop friendly relations among nations based on respect for the principle of equal rights and self-determination of peoples, and to take other appropriate measures to strengthen universal peace. [8]

Now, if you were to do this, there are four requirements[9] for the creation of an independent state. I submit—as I'll point out as I go through the analysis—that the Native Hawaiian people, Kanaka Maoli, have all the requirements you need to go ahead and do this if this is your choice, this is your decision.

First, we need a fixed territory, and clearly we have the Hawaiian Archipelago.

Second, a population, a distinguishable population of people, the Native Hawaiians, those who would trace their ancestry back before the appearance of Europeans on these lands.

Third, a government, and here you have your communal structures, the Kupunas—Kekuni Blaisdell, my friend—and the Kupuna Councils, that you've traditionally had. You don't need a government along the lines of the Federal government of the United States or the State of Hawaii to have a government. Rather what you need is a way to organize your people to govern your relations among each other, and clearly you have that.

And fourth, the capacity to enter into international relations, to deal with other states, and to keep your commitments. As I understand it, there are already states in the Western Pacific region that support the Native Hawaiian people and probably would be prepared to give you diplomatic recognition as an independent state if this is your desire. And I also suspect, like the Palestinians, there would be a large number of states—certainly in the Third World, that have come out of a colonial situation, in Latin America, Africa, and Asia—that would also be prepared to recognize you as an independent state, and enter into diplomatic relations with you. Whether you would someday be allowed into the United Nations of course would depend on the U.S. veto, but even there, the U.S. veto does not go on forever. Eventually they lifted the veto on the admission of Vietnam to the United Nations, despite the enormous hostility towards the people of Vietnam, and Vietnam became a member nation of the United Nations Organization.[10]

So that being said as preliminary, introductory remarks, I'd like to go through the Public Law on a line-by-line basis and give you my analysis of it. And indeed I would encourage all of you, as Native Hawaiians, to study this. It makes what happened to you very clear. And this is now officially recognized as a matter of United States domestic law. You should be able to take this law any time you're in court and haul it out and show it to the judge and the jury, and say, "This is the law; this is what has happened to me and my people, and I am basing my conduct, whatever I am doing, on the basis of this law. It cannot be denied any more." As a litigator before the International Court of Justice, I would be able to take this law to the World Court and say, "The United States government has now officially conceded that it illegally invaded and occupied the Kingdom of Hawaii, and for this reason the native people of Hawaii would be entitled to a restoration of their independent status as a sovereign nation state, to go back to what they were before the U.S. invasion, to undo the damage that had been done."

Now this is styled as an apology, and one might say: Yes, an apology is certainly here and it's long overdue. But it's also not enough. When a government commits a severe violation of international law, as happened here, they just don't apologize and walk away. Damages are required, reparations, and—in extraordinary circumstances—restitution, that is to return the situation to what it was before the violation.[11] Especially when you have a treaty violation and in the case of the Kingdom of

Hawaii, there were three treaties on point, in law, with the United States government that were violated by means of the invasion. This violated international law at the time, the basic principle—*pacta sunt servanda*—treaties must be obeyed.[12] It even violated the terms of the United States Constitution at that time. Treaties were the "supreme law of the land,"[13] and the invasion and annexation of Hawaii in violation of those treaties not only violated international law, but the United States Constitution itself.

So an apology is certainly a start, but we really now have to deal with the consequences. What are the implications of this apology, of this law? And that is the topic I am addressing here tonight: what might be some of the implications of this law. And indeed, the implications, I submit, depend on what you, the Hawaiian people, are going to make of this. It is for you to decide the implications, not the Congress, not the State of Hawaii government, but the Hawaiian people, pursuant to your right of self-determination. What will be the implications of this, as you see it? What do you want?

It's clear then, the U.S. admitted in the law that they overthrew the Kingdom of Hawaii.[14] A clearly illegal act, under the standards of international law in existence at that time, no question or doubt about it.

In a meeting this morning, I was speaking with Judge Nakea[15] on behalf of the Graces,[16] and he said: Well, yes, but in the United States law, the United States government has always been able to extinguish the right of native peoples, and the Supreme Court has seen nothing wrong with that. I said: Well, that might be the case with respect to Native Americans living in the United States, but here in Hawaii you're in a very different situation. You had these three treaties, one of which was a Treaty of Friendship, and Commerce and Navigation,[17] that established good relations between two sovereign states, and they violated that, too. And this issue, a treaty of this nature, came up most recently in the World Court in the *Nicaragua*[18] case, when the World Court condemned the United States government for violating a Treaty of Friendship, Commerce, and Navigation, for mining the harbors in Nicaragua. And certainly the World Court can do the same thing for overthrowing a monarch, and overthrowing and destroying an entire sovereign nation state.

And here then you have the Congress of the United States of America admitting that in one of its own laws. And that's very clear, this admission, what we lawyers call an "admission against interest." They have admitted what they did, and they have then opened this Pandora's Box. How should this be remedied? And again the one point to keep in mind here is that it is now for the Hawaiian people to decide the appropriate remedy, not the Congress. They're the criminals. They've admitted what they've done now, for the last one hundred years—and that the American presence, then, in Hawaii, for the last hundred years, has been nothing more than an illegal, colonial, military occupation regime.

The next sentence goes on—and here remember it's important when reading through this Act, the so-called "whereas clauses": these are official findings of fact and law, by the Congress of the United States. These findings bind all state and federal courts here in Hawaii. And again as I was pointing out this morning to Judge Nakea with respect to the case of Mike and Sondra Grace, the court and judges are bound by these findings of fact. They can no longer be contested or denied. They're stuck with them.

> Whereas, prior to the arrival of the first Europeans in 1778, the Native Hawaiian people lived in a highly organized, self-sufficient, subsistent social system, based on communal land tenure, with a sophisticated language, culture, and religion. [19]

That concedes that Native Hawaiians at that time and as of today still have the one requirement for an international state, which I mentioned: a government. You had a means to govern yourselves as a people. Congress has effectively conceded it right there. It still is in existence today. And this is a type, a system of government, that is historically separate and apart from the State of Hawaii or the United States Federal government. It is still there, it still works today. I've seen it since I arrived here on Sunday with my visits with Bumpy and the Ohana Council—the people of Hawaii providing shelter, food, housing, education, dispute settlement procedures, and mechanisms. The types of things that you did a hundred years ago before the U.S. invasion, to some extent you're still doing today, and it would simply be a question of expanding those types of functions that you provide to your own people.

In the case of Palestine, this is building the state from the ground up, where the Palestinian people rejected participation, acquiescence, collaboration, with Israeli military occupation forces, and proceeded to provide social services to their own people: health, education, judges, dispute settlement, whatever.[20] That is building the state from the ground up. That's how you build a state. No one is going to give it to you. I doubt very seriously that the U.S. Congress tomorrow is just going to pass a statute and give you a state and say, "Here." Rather you go out and say: We're creating our state. There it is, and we ask you to recognize the state, and then the consequences from there.

The next sentence:

> Whereas, a unified monarchical government of the Hawaiian Islands was established in 1810 under Kamehameha I, the first King of Hawaii. [21]

Again, Congress admitted, you had a government. You had a state. It was there. It was viable and functioning. It was internationally active. This was not a situation that the U.S. government maintains with respect to Native Americans.[22] Now here they're wrong, too. They maintain that Native Americans did not have a state type structure that they had to recognize, because it was somewhat different from the structures of government that Europeans brought to the North American continent.[23] We know they're wrong. The Native Americans did have a governing structure. It's just the Europeans didn't want to recognize it, and wanted to steal the land.[24]

But putting that aside, you're in a very different situation here from Native Americans. Now Congress has conceded what they will not concede for the Native Americans[25]—that you had a state, that it was a state just like any other state in existence at that time—just like the United States of America—and was entitled to as much respect and dignity. And Congress has now conceded this point.

That's why when I read in the newspaper on Monday about

this recent visit to Hawaii by the Secretary of the Interior Bruce Babbitt, and his question, "Should Native Hawaiians become treated by the federal government like the Native Americans?" My response to reading that is, "Why would Native Hawaiians want to do that?" Those of you who had a chance to view the tape of the San Francisco Tribunal—and I encourage those who haven't seen it to watch it, Kekuni has it, Kekuni participated—you'll see that Native Americans are up against genocide and extermination. That's the policy of the federal government with respect to Native Americans. So I don't understand why Native Hawaiians would want to buy into such a system and be treated in the system in a way that ultimately would lead to your extermination. And that's certainly the way large numbers of Native Americans see it. Addressing that was the purpose of the San Francisco Tribunal. Again, I encourage you, if you haven't seen it, have a look at that tape. Whatever you do, I would certainly caution you against seeking the same type of treatment that the federal government has doled out to the Native Americans, because we know where that will lead.

Moreover, on the basis of this statute, you're entitled to a lot more than what they give the Native Americans. And that's not to say that, in my opinion, the Native Americans aren't also entitled to establish themselves as independent nations, if that is their desire. But the difference here is that your right to do this, the predicate to do this, has now been recognized by the United States Congress itself,[26] whereas Congress has never recognized this for Native Americans.[27] I doubt the U.S. Congress ever will, because if they did that, they would eliminate the whole basis of pseudo-legitimacy upon which the United States Congress rests, as it relates to land, title, and everything else. I doubt very seriously that they'll want to do that.

The next paragraph:

> Whereas, from 1826 to 1893, the United States recognized the independence of the Kingdom of Hawaii, extended full and complete diplomatic recognition to the Hawaiian Government, and entered into treaties and conventions with the Hawaiian monarchs to govern commerce and navigation in 1826, 1842, 1849, 1875, and 1887. [28]

Note they didn't put the word "friendship" in there, they wanted to delete it, although the treaty covered friendship, commerce, and navigation. So here they're admitting that the invasion, overthrow, occupation, annexation, starting in 1893 on up, violated all these treaties, violated basic norms of international law, even those in existence at that time, which was a pretty bad time, one must admit. You had states going to war, people killing each other, the strong doing what they will, the weak suffering what they must, pretty much like today in the New World Order.

But again, here is the United States Congress taking this position: Yes, this behavior was illegal under international law even in accordance with the minimal standards at that time. And again this distinguishes the case of the Native Hawaiians from the Native Americans, where they have yet to admit that there was anything wrong under international law with the way they treated the Native Americans. All the Supreme Court cases say: Well, this is just the right of conquest, and those were the rules in existence at that time.[29] But what the U.S. Congress is saying here is: No, this was not just a question of right of conquest, but of treaty violations. They were violated. What the U.S. did violated international law. It even violated the terms of the United States Constitution at the time where treaties were the "supreme law of the land."[30] So again, legally you're in a much different, much better situation than Native Americans.

The section on the Congregational Church—well, as I understand it, there is an attempt being made to have reconciliation. I'll skip over that one.[31]

> Whereas, on January 14, 1893, John L. Stevens... the United States Minister, assigned to the sovereign and independent Kingdom of Hawaii conspired with a small group of non-Hawaiian residents of the Kingdom of Hawaii, including citizens of the United States, to overthrow the indigenous and lawful Government of Hawaii. [32]

So again, they concede that the government of the Kingdom of Hawaii was the lawful government at that time, and that an official agent of the United States government conspired to overthrow the government of Hawaii. So the United States government is bound by the actions of its agent, of its Minister.[33] And so they can't say, "He did it, and later on we condemned what he did." You know the President did shed a crocodile tear or two over what he did, did he not, right? There was a statement. That is not enough. Of course it isn't. If the minister did it, it is just the same as the President doing it. There is no difference. The President was bound by the actions of his minister. The United States government was bound by the actions of its minister. Thus, it was the United States government that conspired to overthrow the lawful government of the Kingdom of Hawaii. Again, an internationally illegal act at the time it was done.

The next paragraph continues,

> Whereas, in pursuance of the conspiracy to overthrow the Government of Hawaii, the United States Minister and the naval representatives of the United States caused armed naval forces of the United States to invade the sovereign Hawaiian nation on January 16, 1893, and to position themselves near the Hawaiian government buildings and the Iolani Palace to intimidate Queen Liliuokalani and her Government. [34]

Notice the use of the word "invade." Today we like to use euphemisms such as "incursion," right? That's another word for invasion. But here they call an invasion an invasion, right? That's what it was, a clearly illegal act, an invasion in violation of treaties and international agreements, an invasion in violation of international law, and of the United States Constitution, the overthrow of a lawful government. And again, under international law when you have a violation of treaties of this magnitude, the World Court has ruled that the only appropriate remedy is restitution.[35] Damages are not enough, reparations are not enough–that is the payment of money–or giving you an island over here and saying, "Here, you can have that island." No, restitution, to restore what you once had, that is, the Kingdom of Hawaii, your independent nation state: this is the appropriate remedy, if that is what you want, for what was done.

Now it goes on from here, reciting the sorry history of what happened, the establishment of the provisional government.[36] Well, that government is not entitled to any legitimacy at all. It was imposed by raw, naked, brutal military force, at the point of a bayonet, in an exercise of gunboat diplomacy by the United States Government, just as was practiced in many other countries. Only here now Congress is finally admitting this.

And again, as the Public Law is pointing out in the next paragraph, the establishment of this provisional government was done without the consent of the Native Hawaiian people or the lawful government of Hawaii and violated all of these international treaties and agreements.[37] So under international law, you would not call this a provisional government: I certainly wouldn't call it that. You would call it a government of military occupation. And certainly I would suggest that would be an appropriate way to think about it. That is, you had military forces here along with a civilian arm of the military occupying regime.

You see the same thing today in the occupied Palestinian lands, where you have the Israeli occupying forces who have then set up a civilian arm of their military occupational authorities to administer the civil affairs of the Palestinian people.[38] These matters, by the way, are currently the subject of the negotiations between the P.L.O. and Israel, concerning the withdrawal of (1) the civilian military occupation arm, and then of (2) the military occupation forces themselves.[39] And indeed the September 13, 1993 Agreement signed by Arafat and Rabin calls for the dissolution of the civilian occupation arm and then the withdrawal of the military occupation forces themselves.[40]

So I submit that this "provisional government" is really the civilian arm of a military occupation force, and that then is the predecessor to the current government of Hawaii that administers you today. Again, following the implications of the Public Law, that the state government of Hawaii occupies a similar position. And then of course you have federal occupying military forces here keeping it in power. Again, this is somewhat similar to the arrangement in Palestinian lands.

We then come to the very famous statement by your Queen:

> That I yield to the superior force of the United States of America... [41]

and you are aware of the rest of the language. Well, she made it very clear here that this statement and her later abdication were procured under duress and force. In other words, it could not be treated by anyone as a valid surrender of sovereignty by the Native Hawaiian people at all. And she made that very clear in this language. So in other words she was simply bowing to superior power, but not as a matter of right or of law. I used similar wording myself in the *Bosnia* case in the World Court,[42] where I pointed out in a file communicating with the World Court, that the so-called Owen-Stoltenberg Plan[43] to partition the Republic of Bosnia and Herzegovina, was concluded, or arguably still might be concluded, by means of threats and duress, compulsion and coercion, and therefore was invalid, would be invalid under international law and the Vienna Convention on the Law of Treaties.[44] This type of behavior still goes on today. But your Queen, a very powerful person, made it clear that she was simply yielding to superior force, and thus she preserved the rights of her people for the future: their right of self-determination, their right to restoration of their sovereignty.

The law goes on, where Congress admits:

> ...without the active support and intervention by the United States diplomatic and military representatives the insurrection against the Government of Queen Liliuokalani would have failed for lack of popular support and insufficient arms. [45]

I was reading this recent little letter by the fellow [Thurston Twigg-Smith] who traces his ancestry back to one of the missionaries who pulled this overthrow off, who is presently saying: We should stop all this debate, these are real genuine patriots, et cetera, et cetera, and of course they were entitled to do what they did.[46] Apparently he didn't bother to read the new Public Law. While he can say whatever he wants, Congress has now made it very clear what happened. Twigg-Smith can argue till the cows come home but this is now the law. He'd better read it. And in fact Congress has condemned what his ancestors had done. And now the simple question is: Where do the Native Hawaiian people want to go from here?

Well, again:

> Whereas, on February 1, 1893, the United States Minister raised the American flag and proclaimed Hawaii to be a protectorate of the United States. [47]

Well, of course that's nonsense. They didn't protect anything, did they? There was no need to protect Hawaii, what, from itself, from its own people? Who was threatening Hawaii at that time? It was the United States. They needed protection from the United States, so this is absurd. It's entitled to no legal validity at all at the time, or even now, and that's basically what Congress is admitting.

According to a finding by the Blount Report, the presidentially established investigation conducted by Congressmen James Blount into the events surrounding the insurrection and overthrow:

> ...the United States diplomatic and military representatives had abused their authority and were responsible for the change in government. [48]

Again, they admit that they had acted illegally under international law. But an admission is not enough. The implication, then, of these admissions, by Congress, by the Blount Committee, is that there must be restitution.[49] The Hawaiian people have a right to be returned to the situation they were in as of January 16, 1893. This is their right if that's what the Hawaiian people want. The U.S. government disciplined the Minister Stevens and forced him to resign his commission. Well, they should have done that, of course they should have, but that should not have been the end of the process. The overthrow should have been reversed. They had the authority to do it. The President could have done it if he had wanted to, he just didn't do it. So this is simply eye-washing. It's nice that the United States finally conceded these points, but it's not enough under international law.

Now I don't know how the Native Hawaiians feel about it. I suspect maybe they'd agree with me that it's certainly not enough. Where it should lead from here you know is another issue. Again I'm trying to point out line-by-line that this Resolution clears up all these matters, all debate, all argument, and it makes it very clear you have a right of restoration, of restitution, to proclaim your state. And you don't need the permission of Congress to do this. Congress might not like it, but they're kind of stuck with their own law, are they not?

President Cleveland, in his message to Congress of 1893, admitted all this, saying the overthrow of the government of Hawaii was:

> ...an act of war, committed with the participation of a diplomatic representative of the United States and without authority of Congress. [50]

He was clearly admitting that this was illegal behavior of the most heinous type. A "substantial wrong has thus been done," calling for the restoration of the Hawaiian monarchy.[51] Now of course the fact that it wasn't done doesn't change the legal situation. Today, a hundred years later, you have a right to restore it yourselves, if that's what you want to do. You don't need to petition Congress to do it. Congress has given you everything you need right here to do it, if that's what you want to do. And the United Nations Charter provides the rest of the authority to do it.[52]

I won't go through all of the paragraphs here because I take it all of you have read it. The Newlands Joint Resolution[53] provided for the annexation of Hawaii. Where's the authority for this? There is none. The United States invaded the country, stole the land, displaced the government, and now they annex it. This issue was addressed by the Nuremberg Tribunal in 1945, where the Nazi government tried to maintain that some of the annexations of foreign territory that it had undertaken before and during the Second World War were entitled to legal recognition. The Nuremberg Tribunal itself in 1945 said, "No, annexations are invalid, prior to the conclusion of a peace treaty."[54] The United States government and the President conceded they had engaged in acts of war, that they are occupying your country. That puts them at war with your people.[55] Now they may have annexed Hawaii, but the annexation has no validity under international law. If as part of the peace treaty between Hawaii and the United States you want to concede some land to them, that's up to you, that's your choice. Or if you want to give them operating facilities for a base upon the payment of funds and rent or other compensation, that's for you to decide. But now they have effectively, in this law, invalidated their entire annexation. The whole legal basis for it has now been invalidated by the U.S. Congress itself.

As I was pointing out to Judge Nakea this morning, if the annexation of the land is invalid, then where does the title come from, who has title to the land? It's the Native Hawaiian people who retain title to the lands of Hawaii, as a matter of international law. Not the federal government, not the state government, but the people themselves. That's the implication here, certainly as I read this section, as an international lawyer. And again these findings of fact and conclusions of law are now officially set forth by Congress. What are the implications then of these findings of fact and conclusions of law? Let us spell it out again, line-by-line, what the implications are.

> Whereas, through the Newlands Resolution, the self-declared Republic of Hawaii ceded sovereignty over the Hawaiian Islands to the United States. [56]

We've already determined that the so-called Republic of Hawaii was the civilian occupying arm of a military occupation authority. But again the Republic of Hawaii never had sovereignty over the Hawaiian Islands.[57] Military occupation forces, even though they are there and are present, do not exercise sovereignty over the territories they occupy. Sovereignty remains in the hands of the displaced sovereign. This is black-letter international law.[58] This is the issue at stake in the Middle East peace negotiations between the Israelis and Palestinians. The Israelis do not have sovereignty over the West Bank, the Gaza strip, and East Jerusalem. They're a military occupation authority. They exercise administrative powers, but they do not have sovereignty. They never had. The sovereignty remains in the hands of the Palestinian people, and they have proclaimed a state. Again I submit there is a parallel here for Native Hawaiian people. Sovereignty resides in your hands. This so-called "Republic" never had sovereignty to cede to the United States. That's pretty clear just reading through the resolution and moving one step forward from the analysis set forth here.

> Whereas, the Republic of Hawaii also ceded 1,800,000 acres of crown, government, and public lands of the Kingdom of Hawaii, without the consent of or compensation to the Native Hawaiian people or their sovereign government. [59]

Once again, the government of the Republic of Hawaii was a military occupation authority, the civilian arm, without any sovereign claims to the land under the laws of military occupation, the laws of war. There was nothing to cede. They had no power to cede anything. So the title to the land rested and still rests, under international law, with the Native Hawaiian people.

Again, as I was trying to point this out this morning to Judge Nakea: How can it be said that the Graces trespassed on their own land? You can't trespass on your own land. If it is your land, the trespassers then become the State of Hawaii, and the land developers, and the golf courses, and the resorts. So what this statute does is completely turn the whole situation around on its head. It now changes the whole way that these authorities should be looking at the matter. They're the trespassers and the criminals. You, the Native Hawaiians, are simply asserting your rights under international law. And now this arrangement, as it were, this reversal of positions, between who is the criminal and who is the victim, who is asserting their rights and who is violating their rights, has been effectively conceded by Congress.

I encourage all Native Hawaiians to know what are your rights. Get a copy, a little hand copy of the Universal Declaration of Human Rights,[60] and carry it around with you. Your rights are in here. With respect to what Bumpy Kanahele and his people are doing out on the beaches, in the settlements, Article 25,

> Everyone has the right to a standard of living adequate for the health and well-being of himself and of his family, including food, clothing, housing, medical care and necessary social services... [61]

They have a right to have housing, that's clear. The State of Hawaii has no right to throw you out of your own homes, even if those homes are nothing more than tents on a beach, they're still your homes, and on your beach. Where is their right now, if they ever had any, after the passage of this Act? I don't see it. It's no longer there. The same with respect to the attempt to destroy your temples. Places of worship, Article 18 of the Declaration,

> Everyone has the right to freedom of thought, conscience, and religion; this right includes freedom... to manifest his religion or belief in teaching, practice, worship, and observance. [62]

So where is the right of the State of Hawaii, or a real estate developer, or a resort developer, to destroy any of your temples, when these are your temples, this is your land, your right to worship is guaranteed in the Universal Declaration? I don't see that right and indeed it will be very hard for them to argue that right now that this law has been passed. I won't go through the applicability of all the rights set out in the Universal Declaration of Human Rights to the activities of Native Hawaiians here in their relations with the state and federal governments. Again I'd encourage you to get copies from Amnesty International. They have them available. Read through it, and understand what your rights are, and proceed to assert them in your dealings with the state and federal government.

> Whereas, the Congress...annexed Hawaii as part of the United States, and vested title to the lands in Hawaii in the United States. [63]

Clearly illegal. We've already seen it. The annexation was invalid. The United States can't get title from the Republic of Hawaii because that body, established by the U.S. itself, never had title in the first place. It had no sovereignty. It was nothing more than a military occupation power, and a military occupation power cannot validly transfer title to land. Again, this is black-letter international law.[64] That is why today the United States government condemns the settlements in occupied Palestinian land. Settlements are illegal. The occupying power can't transfer title or sell land legally. I mean they can do it, but that doesn't make it lawful. The sale or transfer is invalid. It is illegal. An occupying power can't sell land, because they don't control title or sovereignty. They can administer, but that's all, arguably, they can do. In theory, they're obliged to leave, not to stay.

> Whereas, the Newlands Resolution effected the transaction between the Republic of Hawaii and the United States government. [65]

Again, the Newlands Resolution is entitled to no validity at all, since it's based on an illegal invasion, violation of treaties, violation of the principle of *pacta sunt servanda*.[66] We could be here all night discussing all the violations of law that accrued as a result of this.

Not only that, they admit,

> Whereas, the indigenous Hawaiian people never directly relinquished their claims to inherent sovereignty as a people or over their national lands to the United States, either through their monarchy or through a plebiscite or referendum. [67]

This gets back to the question of what happened, back in, what 1959, right? What validity was that Newlands Resolution entitled to? Well now Congress is saying: None! And I would say: even after this, none, because you didn't have a plebiscite conducted by the United Nations Organization itself, which would have been a requirement for the Hawaiian people to accede to statehood in the United States, if their lands had been occupied by the U.S. and held in trusteeship under Article 73 of the U.N. Charter.[68] The U.S. didn't do that. So Congress is effectively conceding now that the so-called vote to become a "state" of the United States in 1959 is meaningless, as a matter of international law and United States domestic law. So you're not bound by it. Rather I'm suggesting you're now free to determine your own fate pursuant to the principle of self-determination in Article 1, paragraph 2 of the United Nations Charter.[69]

Let me skip down again.

> Whereas, the long-range economic and social changes in Hawaii over the nineteenth and early twentieth centuries have been devastating to the population and to the health and well-being of the Hawaiian people. [70]

Well that's an understatement. The Hawaiian people have been subjected to the international crime of genocide, as determined and defined by the 1948 Genocide Convention,[71] and the 1987 Genocide Convention Implementation Act, the Proxmire Resolution.[72] That is clear. That was one of the findings of the San Francisco Tribunal. That was one of the key findings of the Tribunal held here this summer concerning Hawaii [Ka Ho'okolokolonui Kanaka Maoli]. And I submit, having argued genocide myself to the International Court of Justice, and having convinced them that genocide is going on in Bosnia-Herzegovina,[73] I personally would have no difficulty at all in convincing the World Court that genocide has been practiced by the United States government against Native Hawaiians. Now, that's bad enough, but where does that lead you? I submit where it leads you is back to the creation of a State. One of the few and only protections a people have from being exterminated and ceasing to exist when faced with genocide, is to have their own state and ultimately United Nations membership, which registers their existence and provides them access to the protections of international law.

Today the situation is being replayed in respect to the Bosnians. The Bosnians do have a state and they do have U.N. membership, which is the one thing they have keeping them from going the way of history.[74] And the Palestinians recognize this too: that they had to proclaim a state, in order to protect themselves from being annihilated. So a state, an independent sovereign nation state is one way a people who are threatened with extermination by means of genocide can attempt to protect themselves. According to the statistics that Kekuni Blaisdell presented to the San Francisco Tribunal, the Native Hawaiian people are threatened with extinction by the year 2040. So this is something that has to be given very serious consideration. What is the best way to protect the existence of your people, as a people? Is it to accept the same status as Native Americans, which I guess Secretary Babbitt is considering graciously giving you? Or is it to proclaim your own state, and then ultimately seek international recognition and finally U.N. membership? Again, this is for you to decide. You have to consider the alternatives because ultimately it's your future and that of your children and your children's children that is at stake.

Now in the final "whereas" clause, they say,

> ...it is proper and timely for the Congress...to acknowledge the historic significance of the illegal overthrow of the Kingdom of Hawaii. [75]

Before then they only talked about an overthrow, they didn't concede it was illegal, although it violated all these treaties; now they say it is illegal. So in other words, they're agreeing with what I'm telling you. It was illegal. If you had any doubt, now even Congress is agreeing. It was an illegal overthrow. It had no validity at all. So accordingly, the fruits of this overthrow are entitled to no recognition as being valid today. And that calls into question title to all the land here. Whose land is it? Well, from what Congress seems to be saying to me is: it's the land of the Native Hawaiian people.

Then they talk about reconciliation efforts, that they support the reconciliation efforts.[76] Well, of course I'm in favor of reconciliation. But there's more to it than that. Again, under international law, if you have a violation of this nature the appropriate remedy is not simply reconciliation, apology or reparations, but restitution.[77] That is, to set right the harm that had been done. To restore the situation to what it had been before the violation in 1893. And there is a very famous case decided by the World Court, the *Chorzow Factory*[78] case, which would be the authority for this. So in other words, sure, have reconciliation. But what about restoration? That clearly is what you're entitled to.

Now we get to this Section 1, Acknowledgment and Apology.[79] Again, they repeat, "Illegal overthrow," so it's not simply me interpreting the significance of the various whereas clauses, but now the fact that this was an illegal overthrow is recognized in the operative provision of the statute: "Resolved by the Senate and House of Representatives of the United States of America, in Congress assembled," and signed by the President.[80]

> ...acknowledges the historical significance of this event which resulted in the suppression of the inherent sovereignty of the Native Hawaiian People. [81]

Notice what they're saying. The Native Hawaiian people still have sovereignty. The sovereignty *inheres* in you. And now it is for you to decide what to do with this sovereignty. Because the state of Hawaii, the federal government, are, as I said, the civilian arms of the military occupation authority. And military occupation authorities do not have sovereign powers. The sovereignty resides in the people. And that is clearly the implication of Section 1 of the operative provision of the statute.

Paragraph 3 apologizes for the overthrow, "with the participation of agents and citizens of the United States."[82] Again, if you had any doubt about what I was telling you before, about the U.S. government being responsible for the actions of its ministers, they've now called these people "agents." So as such, their conduct, their illegal conduct, binds the United States government, which means the United States government then, is under an obligation to undo the harm that was done. But even if they don't, the Native Hawaiian people themselves have a right to act to undo that harm. And again if you doubt that, the rest of the sentence says, "and the deprivation of the rights of Native Hawaiians to self-determination..."[83] So in other words, Congress has conceded that the Native Hawaiian people have a right to self-determination. What does that right include? Well, as I said, the right of self-determination of peoples under the U.N. Charter means a right to a state of your own and to membership ultimately someday in the United Nations Organization,[84] just like the 188 other states that are currently members of the United Nations today.

Paragraph 4 expresses its commitment to acknowledge the ramifications of the overthrow.[85] What are the ramifications? Well, that is the subject of my discussion tonight. If you followed the analysis that I presented before, then I have put forward here what I believe are the ramifications, the implications, of the overthrow of the Kingdom of Hawaii. Now, whether that's the direction you want to go, that is up to you, for you to decide, not me.

And then again finally in the definitional Section 2, where they talk about Native Hawaiians, ostensibly stating who they are:

> ...any individual who is a descendant of the aboriginal

> people, who, prior to 1778, occupied and exercised sovereignty, in the area that now constitutes the state of Hawaii. [86]

Again, this is affirming that the native people of Hawaii were and by implication still are the sovereign authority in these lands, not the present state government, not the federal government, but the Native Hawaiian people themselves. Well, based then on this public law, and going through it line-by-line, I would express the opinion that today the Kanaka Maoli have the right to exercise self-determination as a people in accordance with the U.N. Charter, and proclaim an independent state, if that is your desire, join the world community of states as an independent nation state. This also means that you have the right to determine your political status, your type of governmental organization if you wish to govern yourselves through customary systems. And to freely pursue your economic, social, cultural development in accordance with Article I of the International Covenant on Civil and Political Rights and the International Covenant on Economic, Social and Cultural Rights.[87] The United States government is party to that first treaty. That treaty also recognizes the right of Native Hawaiians to freely dispose of your natural wealth and resources, without prejudice to obligations arising out of international economic cooperation. This is your land. These are your natural resources. Whatever powers are exercised by the state and federal governments are those of a colonial occupation military regime. But the sovereignty still resides in the hands of the Native Hawaiian people. You have the territory necessary for a state: the first requirement. The Hawaiian Archipelago, the lands that you had before the invasion of 1893. You would be entitled to claim a 12 mile territorial sea and a 200 mile exclusive economic zone, in accordance with customary international law and the Law of the Sea Treaty of 1982.[88]

The second requirement of an independent state is the people. And, again Congress has recognized the Kanaka Maoli people are a group of people with sovereignty, sovereign powers. You have lived here forever. You are the original inhabitants and occupants of these islands. You have always been in possession of your land. And so you would be entitled to reestablish an independent sovereign nation state in that land. Possession is nine-tenths of the law. You're still here, you're still living in your homes, you are still occupying your land. And it might be true that the state and federal governments are illegally dispossessing you. But you are still holding on, you're still building settlements, you're still occupying it, and you're staying there. And that's all that international law requires, and certainly is your right under the Universal Declaration of Human Rights.[89]

Who would be your citizens? Well certainly the citizens would be those who are descendants of the Kanaka Maoli, who occupied and exercised sovereignty in Hawaii, prior to the Europeans in 1778. You would trace your ancestors back. Again, it would be your right to determine who your citizens are.

I take it you would reject this blood percentage that has been set up by the United States government, reminiscent of Nazi laws that were applied to decide who was Aryan, laws which in turn were patterned on laws in the American South, on miscegenation, related to determining who was a black and who was a white.[90]

The way this is normally done by most states today is that a state is free to determine who its own citizens are. And certainly you would be free to determine that all those who could trace their ancestors back to 1778 would automatically become citizens of the new state.

Now, what about those who are living here who are not able to trace their ancestors back? What about them? Again this is an issue that has confronted several states today. For example, in the Baltics, Lithuania, Latvia and Estonia, where you have large number of Russian citizens left behind as a result of the Russian/Soviet occupation for the last 50 years, which is about half the passage of time that you're dealing with. And the Baltic States, the three of them, have taken different approaches. For a period of time I advised the Republic of Lithuania under President Landsbergis, who was the hero and leader of their independence movement, who then lost an election and the people voted the Communists back in, so I no longer advise them. But they've taken a very generous approach to those Russians who remain, trying to integrate them into their society.[91]

And certainly the Hawaiian state could take the position that you'll set up a procedure to provide citizenship to all people who are habitual residents of the new state of Hawaii as of a certain date, which would mean those who have lived here continuously five years, ten years, whatever cut off point you want—these are also entitled to become citizens of this state on a level of equality with everyone else, but they have to apply for it. It would not be automatic, as would be the case with the Native Hawaiians, who would automatically become citizens.

And again there are precedents here in the way the Palestinians are dealing with this. They too have a diaspora population. You have large numbers of Hawaiians all over the world who had to leave Hawaii. Approaching it this way would enable you to allow all of them too to claim Hawaiian citizenship, if that's what they want to do—to return. The Palestinians did it that way. They set up a state and said: We're setting up a state for all Palestinians everywhere in the world. So in theory those who want to be citizens of the state can make that claim and be admitted. There are also a large number of Jewish settlers living in occupied Palestine. The Palestinians have taken the position that they are prepared to accept a certain number of Jewish settlers as citizens living in their state on a basis of equality with everyone else, provided that they are prepared to be peaceful and law-abiding and to be treated as equals.

So there are precedents for the new state of Hawaii to take a similar position for those non-native Hawaiians who live here, and for saying: We don't want you to leave. We're setting up an inclusive state. We want you to stay. You would simply have to apply for citizenship in the new state. It could be done in a way that they would not have to renounce their U.S. citizenship if that's what the Native Hawaiians decide. That could be a big issue for the current generation of non-native Hawaiians living here. It probably would not be a big issue for the next generation. They would be Hawaiian at birth, entitled to citizenship at birth, and probably whether they would claim U.S. citizenship wouldn't be all that important. But for those who are here who are U.S. citizens it would be possible to allow them to become dual nationals. That is, they would apply for Hawaiian citizenship without having to give up U.S. citizenship. And this would be fully consistent with United States law. I was born in the United States, but I applied for Irish citizenship. My family's Irish, and I have Irish citizenship and an Irish passport. The Irish have been subjected to genocide too. We know what it's all about. We are a diaspora people, too. We have people all over the world. And so we have an inclusive form of citizenship that allows people to claim it without having to give up whatever other citizenship they have as well. The Native Hawaiian state could approach the question of citizenship in a similar way.

I've already discussed that the system of government— the third requirement that you would need for an independent state—and I believe you have it. You have your Kupuna system. As I said, Congress has recognized, in the language I quoted to you,

> ...a highly organized, self-sufficient, subsistent social system based on communal land tenure, with a sophisticated language, culture, and religion. [92]

That's all you need, and you have that. So you would simply work that out, the implications of that system on a state basis, to serve as the new Hawaiian state's governing system. That would be the way the new Hawaiian state would be governed, not the current situation as you see it today.

And finally the last requirement—the capacity to enter into international relations. And again here, I think that if you were to declare an independent state you would probably obtain recognition in that capacity from a fairly large number of states. I could not predict the number of states that would recognize you. I don't know. You would have the same problems in the creation of the Palestinian state. We didn't know how many states would recognize the Palestinian state back in August of 1988, before it was created.[93] But here it is December of 1993, and there are 125 states that recognize the state of Palestine. And someday hopefully the state of Israel will recognize the state of Palestine. The state of Palestine already recognizes the state of Israel, and you can have peace and reconciliation between those two peoples as well.

I could not predict how long this would take, what would be the consequences, how many states will recognize you, but I take it that the plight of the Hawaiian people is generally well known in the world, and there's a great deal sympathy. For a variety of reasons the Palestinians have had an uphill struggle and battle in obtaining that recognition. So it might be that you would be able to obtain recognition quickly. And especially if you pursue this process in accordance with principles of peaceful, non-violent struggle. And I submit that's the most effective technique you have today. If you doubt me, you should read Gandhi's book, *Satyagraha*, Non-Violent Civil Resistance.[94] It's about 300 pages long and explains how Gandhi threw the mighty British Empire out of India without using force. People power, that's what we call it today. I submit that the Native Hawaiian people would be able to do the same thing, moving in this direction and adopting the techniques of peaceful, non-violent action, which is what Gandhi called for.

This concludes the formal comments I had to make this evening. Again, this is presented not as a solution to any problems. My assignment here tonight as I understood it was to sketch, briefly, one outline, one alternative, that the Native Hawaiian people can consider, among other alternatives that are available to you. Obviously you could tell by some of the comments I've made, that I had some problems with a few of the other alternatives that have been presented to you. But ultimately it is your choice to make, not the choice of the United States Congress, not the choice of the State of Hawaii—with all due respect to the Commissioners here. It is the choice of the Native Hawaiian people. They have the right to self-determination, they have inherent sovereignty, and that fact has now even been recognized by the United States Congress itself. So it's no longer just me up here as a law professor giving you an opinion as a law professor. But rather the opinion I'm giving you tonight is based up these formal findings of fact and law by the United States Congress.

Thank you very much.

APPENDIX:

UNITED STATES PUBLIC LAW 103-150
103d Congress Joint Resolution 19
Nov. 23, 1993

To acknowledge the 100th anniversary of the January 17, 1893 overthrow of the Kingdom of Hawaii, and to offer an apology to Native Hawaiians on behalf of the United States for the overthrow of the Kingdom of Hawaii.

Whereas, prior to the arrival of the first Europeans in 1778, the Native Hawaiian people lived in a highly organized, self-sufficient, subsistent social system based on communal land tenure with a sophisticated language, culture, and religion;

Whereas, a unified monarchical government of the Hawaiian Islands was established in 1810 under Kamehameha I, the first King of Hawaii;

Whereas, from 1826 until 1893, the United States recognized the independence of the Kingdom of Hawaii, extended full and complete diplomatic recognition to the Hawaiian Government, and entered into treaties and conventions with the Hawaiian monarchs to govern commerce and navigation in 1826, 1842, 1849, 1875, and 1887;

Whereas, the Congregational Church (now known as the United Church of Christ), through its American Board of Commissioners for Foreign Missions, sponsored and sent more than 100 missionaries to the Kingdom of Hawaii between 1820 and 1850;

Whereas, on January 14, 1893, John L. Stevens (hereafter referred to in this Resolution as the "United States Minister"), the United States Minister assigned to the sovereign and independent Kingdom of Hawaii conspired with a small group of non-Hawaiian residents of the Kingdom of Hawaii, including citizens of the United States, to overthrow the indigenous and lawful Government of Hawaii;

Whereas, in pursuance of the conspiracy to overthrow the Government of Hawaii, the United States Minister and the naval representatives of the United States caused armed naval forces of the United States to invade the sovereign Hawaiian nation on January 16, 1893, and to position themselves near the Hawaiian Government buildings and the Iolani Palace to intimidate Queen Liliuokalani and her Government;

Whereas, on the afternoon of January 17,1893, a Committee of Safety that represented the American and European sugar planters, descendants of missionaries, and financiers deposed the Hawaiian monarchy and proclaimed the establishment of a Provisional Government;

Whereas, the United States Minister thereupon extended diplomatic recognition to the Provisional Government that was formed by the conspirators without the consent of the Native Hawaiian people or the lawful Government of Hawaii and in violation of treaties between the two nations and of international law;

Whereas, soon thereafter, when informed of the risk of bloodshed with resistance, Queen Liliuokalani issued the following statement yielding her authority to the United States Government rather than to the Provisional Government:

> I Liliuokalani, by the Grace of God and under the Constitution of the Hawaiian Kingdom, Queen, do hereby solemnly protest against any and all acts done against myself and the Constitutional Government of the Hawaiian Kingdom by certain persons claiming to have established a Provisional Government of and for this Kingdom.
>
> That I yield to the superior force of the United States of America whose Minister Plenipotentiary, His Excellency John L. Stevens, has caused United States troops to be landed at Honolulu and declared that he would support the Provisional Government.
>
> Now to avoid any collision of armed forces, and perhaps the loss of life, I do this under protest and impelled by said force yield my authority until such time as the Government of the United States shall, upon facts being presented to it, undo the action of its representatives and reinstate me in the authority which I claim as the Constitutional Sovereign of the Hawaiian Islands.
>
> Done at Honolulu this 17th day of January, A.D. 1893.;

Whereas, without the active support and intervention by the United States diplomatic and military representatives, the insurrection against the Government of Queen Liliuokalani would have failed for lack of popular support and insufficient arms;

Whereas, on February 1, 1893, the United States Minister raised the American flag and proclaimed Hawaii to be a protectorate of the United States;

Whereas, the report of a Presidentially established investigation conducted by former Congressman James Blount into the events surrounding the insurrection and overthrow of January 17, 1893, concluded that the United States diplomatic and military representatives had abused their authority and were responsible for the change in government;

Whereas, as a result of this investigation, the United States Minister to Hawaii was recalled from his diplomatic post and the military commander of the United States armed forces stationed in Hawaii was disciplined and forced to resign his commission;

Whereas, in a message to Congress on December 18, 1893, President Grover Cleveland reported fully and accurately on the illegal acts of the conspirators, described such acts as an "act of war, committed with the participation of a diplomatic representative of the United States and without authority of Congress", and acknowledged that by such acts the government of a peaceful and friendly people was overthrown;

Whereas, President Cleveland further concluded that a "substantial wrong has thus been done which a due regard for our national character as well as the rights of the injured people requires we should endeavor to repair" and called for the restoration of the Hawaiian monarchy;

Whereas, the Provisional Government protested President Cleveland's call for the restoration of the monarchy and continued to hold state power and pursue annexation to the United States;

Whereas, the Provisional Government successfully lobbied the Committee on Foreign Relations of the Senate (hereafter referred to in this Resolution as the "Committee") to conduct a new investigation into the events surrounding the overthrow of the monarchy;

Whereas, the Committee and its chairman, Senator John Morgan, conducted hearings in Washington, D.C., from December 27, 1893, through February 26, 1894, in which members of the Provisional Government justified and condoned the actions of the United States Minister and recommended annexation of Hawaii;

Whereas, although the Provisional Government was able to obscure the role of the United States in the illegal overthrow of the Hawaiian monarchy, it was unable to rally the support from two-thirds of the Senate needed to ratify a treaty of annexation;

Whereas, on July 4, 1894, the Provisional Government declared itself to be the Republic of Hawaii;

Whereas, on January 24, 1895, while imprisoned in Iolani Palace, Queen Liliuokalani was forced by representatives of the Republic of Hawaii to officially abdicate her throne;

Whereas, in the 1896 United States Presidential election, William McKinley replaced Grover Cleveland;

Whereas, on July 7, 1898, as a consequence of the Spanish-American War, President McKinley signed the Newlands Joint Resolution that provided for the annexation of Hawaii;

Whereas, through the Newlands Resolution, the self-declared Republic of Hawaii ceded sovereignty over the Hawaiian Islands to the United States;

Whereas, the Republic of Hawaii also ceded 1,800,000 acres of crown, government and public lands of the Kingdom of Hawaii, without the consent of or compensation to the Native Hawaiian people of Hawaii or their sovereign government;

Whereas, the Congress, through the Newlands Resolution, ratified the cession, annexed Hawaii as part of the United States, and vested title to the lands in Hawaii in the United States;

Whereas, the Newlands Resolution also specified that treaties existing between Hawaii and foreign nations were to immediately cease and be replaced by United States treaties with such nations;

Whereas, the Newlands Resolution effected the transaction between the Republic of Hawaii and the United States Government;

Whereas, the indigenous Hawaiian people never directly relinquished their claims to their inherent sovereignty as a people or over their national lands to the United States, either through their monarchy or through a plebiscite or referendum;

Whereas, on April 30, 1900, President McKinley signed the Organic Act that provided a government for the territory of Hawaii and defined the political structure and powers of the newly established Territorial Government and its relationship to the United States;

Whereas, on August 21,1959, Hawaii became the 50th State of the United States;

Whereas, the health and well-being of the Native Hawaiian people is intrinsically tied to their deep feelings and attachment to the land;

Whereas, the long-range economic and social changes in Hawaii over the nineteenth and early twentieth centuries have been devastating to the population and to the health and well-being of the Hawaiian people;

Whereas, the Native Hawaiian people are determined to preserve, develop and transmit to future generations their ancestral territory, and their cultural identity in accordance with their own spiritual and traditional beliefs, customs, practices, language, and social institutions;

Whereas, in order to promote racial harmony and cultural understanding, the Legislature of the State of Hawaii has determined that the year 1993, should serve Hawaii as a year of special reflection on the rights and dignities of the Native Hawaiians in the Hawaiian and the American societies;

Whereas, the Eighteenth General Synod of the United Church of Christ in recognition of the denomination's historical complicity in the illegal overthrow of the Kingdom of Hawaii in 1893 directed the Office of the President of the United Church of Christ to offer a public apology to the Native Hawaiian people and to initiate the process of reconciliation between the United Church of Christ and the Native Hawaiians; and

Whereas, it is proper and timely for the Congress on the occasion of the impending one hundredth anniversary of the event, to acknowledge the historic significance of the illegal overthrow of the Kingdom of Hawaii, to express its deep regret to the Native Hawaiian people, and to support the reconciliation efforts of the State of Hawaii and the United Church of Christ with Native Hawaiians;

Now, therefore, be it

Resolved by the Senate and House of Representatives of the United States of America in Congress assembled,

SECTION 1. ACKNOWLEDGMENT AND APOLOGY.

The Congress -

(1) on the occasion of the 100th anniversary of the illegal overthrow of the Kingdom of Hawaii on January 17, 1893, acknowledges the historical significance of this event which resulted in the suppression of the inherent sovereignty of the Native Hawaiian people;

(2) recognizes and commends efforts of reconciliation initiated by the State of Hawaii and the United Church of Christ with Native Hawaiians;

(3) apologizes to Native Hawaiians on behalf of the people of the United States for the overthrow of the Kingdom of Hawaii on January 17, 1893 with the participation of agents and citizens of the United States, and the deprivation of the rights of Native Hawaiians to self-determination;

(4) expresses its commitment to acknowledge the ramifications of the overthrow of the Kingdom of Hawaii, in order to provide a proper foundation for reconciliation between the United States and the Native Hawaiian people; and

(5) urges the President of the United States to also acknowledge the ramifications of the overthrow of the Kingdom of Hawaii and to support reconciliation efforts between the United States and the Native Hawaiian people.

SEC. 2. DEFINITIONS.

As used in this Joint Resolution, the term "Native Hawaiians" means any individual who is a descendent of the aboriginal people who, prior to 1778, occupied and exercised sovereignty in the area that now constitutes the State of Hawaii.

SEC. 3. DISCLAIMER.

Nothing in this Joint Resolution is intended to serve as a settlement of any claims against the United States.

Approved November 23, 1993

LEGISLATIVE HISTORY - S.J. Res. 19:
SENATE REPORTS: No. 103-125 (Select Comm. on Indian Affairs)
CONGRESSIONAL RECORD, Vol. 139 (1993):
Oct. 27, considered and passed Senate.
Nov. 15, considered and passed House.

ENDNOTES

1 *See* 1993 Haw. Sess. Laws 1009, 1011 (creating the Hawaiian Sovereignty Advisory Commission to advise the Legislature in carrying out the purposes of The Act Relating to Hawaiian Sovereignty).

2 Overthrow of Hawaii Resolution, Pub. L. No. 103-150, 1993 U.S.C.C.A.N. (107 Stat.) 1510.

3 *Id.*

4 *See* John Quigley, *Palestine's Declaration Of Independence: Self-Determination And The Right of The Palestinians to Statehood*, 7 B.U. INT'L L.J. 1 (1989).

5 *Id.*

6 *See, e.g.*, Ved Nanda et. al., *Self Determination: The Case of Palestine*, 82 AM. SOC'Y INT'L L. PROC. 334, 344 (1988).

7 U.N. CHARTER art. 73 ("Members of the United Nations which have or assume responsibilities for the administration of territories whose peoples have not yet attained a full measure of self-government recognize the principle that the interests of the inhabitants of these territories are paramount…").

8 U.N. CHARTER art. 1, ¶ 2.

9 *See* Convention on Rights and Duties of States adopted by the Seventh International Conference of American States, Dec. 26, 1933, 165 L.N.T.S. 19, 25 (listing the requirements for an independent state).

10 *Assembly Opens New Session: Admission of Djibouti, Vietnam*, UN MONTHLY CHRON., Oct. 1977, at 5, 6.

11 Case concerning The Factory at Chorzow, 1928 P.C.I.J. (ser. A) No. 17, at 1 (Sept. 13).

12 Vienna Convention of the Law of Treaties, May 23, 1969, art. 26, 1155 U.N.T.S. 331.

13 *See* U.S. CONST. art. VI, cl. 2 ("all Treaties…shall be The Supreme Law of the Land.")

14 Overthrow of Hawaii Resolution, Pub. L. No. 103-150, 1993 U.S.C.C.A.N. (107 Stat.) 1510, 1512 ("Whereas it is proper and timely for the Congress…to acknowledge the historic significance of the illegal overthrow").

15 The Honorable Clifford L. Nakea serves in the 5th Judicial Circuit of the State of Hawaii, District Court.

16 Michael Grace and Sondra Field built a house in the Anahola Beach Park on the island of Kauai. When ordered to vacate the park by the Hawaiian Homes Commission, they refused, were arrested and then convicted in the Hawaii state courts for trespassing. Their dwelling was destroyed. Grace and Field argued that they had title to the occupied property based on their status as citizens of the independent Nation of Hawaii. The Federal courts, to whom the Graces had turned arguing a denial of due process, refused to acknowledge their property claim. For a full accounting of the case see *Grace v. Drake*, 832 F. Supp. 1399 (D. Haw. 1991), *aff'd*, 1993 U.S. App. LEXIS 24968 (9th Cir. 1993).

17 Treaty of Friendship, Commerce, and Navigation, Dec. 20, 1849, U.S.-Haw., 103 Consol. T.S. 391. *But see* "The cession of the Hawaiian Islands to the United States having been accepted by the resolution approved by the President, July 7, 1898 (30 Stat. 75), the treaties with that country terminated upon the formation of the government for the Islands." William Malloy, TREATIES, CONVENTIONS, INTERNATIONAL ACTS, PROTOCOLS AND AGREEMENTS BETWEEN THE UNITED STATES OF AMERICA AND OTHER POWERS 1776-1909, at 908 (1910).

18 Military & Paramilitary Activities (Nicar v. U.S.), 1986 I.C.J. 4 (June 27).

19 Overthrow of Hawaii Resolution, Pub. L. No. 103-150, 1993 U.S.C.C.A.N. (107 Stat.) 1510.

20 *See* Alon Ben-Meir, *An Intelligent Middle Ground on Which to Build Peace*, CHI. TRIB., Aug. 26, 1987, at 17.

21 Overthrow of Hawaii Resolution, Pub. L. No. 103-150, 1993 U.S.C.C.A.N. (107 Stat.) 1510.

22 *See generally* Markus B. Heyder, Note, *The International Law Commission's Draft Article on State Responsibility: Draft Article 19 and Native American Self-Determination*, 32 COLUM. J. TRANSNAT'L L. 155 (1994); Susan Lope, Note, *Indian Giver: The Illusion of Effective Legal Redress for Native American Land Claims*, 23 SW. U.L. REV. 331 (1994).

23 Lope, *supra* note 22, at 333-34. "Discovery...initiated the inevitable erosion of the Native American nations." *Id.*

24 *See generally* Heyder, *supra* note 22.

25 *See* Wililam J. Murphy, *Jurisdiction – Sovereign Immunity – Business Owned by Native American Nation Granted Sovereign Immunity from Suit Arising From Its Private Off-Reservation Transaction, In Re Greene*, 980 F.2d 590 (9th Cir. 1992), *cert. denied*, 114 S. Ct. 681 (1994), 17 SUFFOLK TRANSNAT'L L.J. 599, 601 n. 16 (1994) (listing cases in which Congress' power to regulate Native Americans was upheld).

26 Overthrow of Hawaii Resolution, Pub. L. No. 103-150, 1993 U.S.C.C.A.N. (107 Stat.) 1510.

27 "In the context of Native American efforts to regain self-determination, the combination of adverse judicial doctrines and the professed plenary power of Congress over Native Americans frustrates any move toward genuine self-determination by Native American peoples." Heyder, *supra* note 22, at 155.

28 Overthrow of Hawaii Resolution, Pub. L. No. 103-150, 1993 U.S.C.C.A.N. (107 Stat.) 1510.

29 *See American Insurance Co. v. Peters*, 26 U.S. (1 Pet.) 511, where Justice Marshall, in an 1828 decision involving the rights of the inhabitants of Florida following the cession of that state from Spain to the United States, states "[t]he usage of the world is, if a nation can be not entirely subdued, to consider the holding of conquered territory as a mere military occupation, until its fate shall be determined at the treaty of peace." *Id.* at 542.

30 U.S. CONST. art. VI, cl. 2.

31 The next section of the law is on the Congregational Church. It is an

attempt at reconciliation and does not need further elaboration.

32 *Id.*

33 *See* Nuclear Tests Case (Austl. v. Fr.) 1974 I.C.J. 252 (Dec. 20), where the International Court of Justice held that:

> It is well recognized that declarations made by way of unilateral acts, concerning legal or factual situations, may have the effect of creating legal obligations. Declarations of this kind may be, and often are, very specific. When it is the intention of the State making the declaration that it should become bound according to its terms, that intention confers on the declaration the character of a legal undertaking, the State being thenceforth legally required to follow a course of conduct consistent with the declaration. An undertaking of this kind, if given publicly, and with an intent to be bound, even though not made within the context of international negotiations, is binding. *Id.* at 267. (holding France bound to statements made by government ministers).

34 Overthrow of Hawaii Resolution, Pub. L. No. 103-150, 1993 U.S.C.C.A.N. (107 Stat.) 1510.

35 Case concerning the Factory at Chorzow, 1928 P.C.I.J. (ser. A.) No. 17, at 47 (Sept. 13).

36 "Whereas, on the afternoon of January 17, 1883, a Committee of Safety that represented the American and European sugar planters, descendants of missionaries, and financiers deposed the Hawaiian monarchy and proclaimed the establishment of a provisional government." Overthrow of Hawaii Resolution, Pub. L. No. 103-150, 1993 U.S.C.C.A.N. (107 Stat.) 1510, 1510-11.

37 "Whereas, the United states minister thereupon extended diplomatic recognition to the Provisional government that was formed by the conspirators without the consent of The Native Hawaiian people or the lawful government of Hawaii and in violation of treaties between the two nations and of international law." Overthrow of Hawaii Resolution, Pub. L. No. 103-150, 1993 U.S.C.C.A.N. (107 Stat.) 1510, 1510-11.

38 *See* J. Timothy McGuire, *International Law and the Administration of Occupied Territories: Two Decades of Israeli Occupation of the West Bank and Gaza Strip*, 8 EMORY INT'L L. REV. 383 (1994).

39 *See* David I. Schulman, *The Israeli-PLO Accord on the Declaration of Principles on Interim Self-Government Arrangements: The First Step Toward Palestinian Self-Determination,* 7 EMORY INT'L L. REV. 793 (Fall 1993); Gumar Halley, *Issues Confronting the Return of Palestinian Arab Refugees After the 1993 Declaration of Principles on Interim Self-Government Arrangements*, 8 GEO. IMMIGR. L.J. 149 (1994).

40 Declaration of Principles on Interim Self-government Arrangements, Sept. 13, 1993, Isr.-P.L.O., art. VI, 32 I.L.M. 1524, 1527. The author served as Legal Advisor to the Palestinian Delegation to the Middle East Peace Negotiations from 1991 to 1993.

41 Overthrow of Hawaii Resolution, Pub. L. No. 103-150, 1993 U.S.C.C.A.N.

(107 Stat.) 1510, 1511.

42 *See* Case Concerning Application of the Convention on the Prevention and Punishment of The Crime of Genocide (Bosnia & Herzegovina v. Yugoslavia), 1993 I.C.J. 325 (Sept. 13). The author served as Bosnia's Agent before the Court.

43 *See* Alan C. Laifer, Note, *Never Again? The 'Concentration Camps' in Bosnia-Herzegovina: A Legal Analysis of Human Rights Abuses*, 2 NEW EUR. L. REV. 159, 187 (Spring 1994). The author served as Legal Advisor to President Izetbegovic and the Members of the Bosnian Presidency during these negotiations during the summer of 1993 in Geneva.

44 "A treaty is void if its conclusion has been procured by the threat or use of force in violation of the principles of international law embodied in the Charter of the United Nations." Vienna Convention of the Law of Treaties, *supra* note 12, at art. 52.

45 Overthrow of Hawaii Resolution, Pub. L. No. 103-150, 1993 U.S.C.C.A.N. (107 Stat.) 1510, 1512.

46 "Honolulu Advertiser publisher Thurston Twigg-Smith, whose grandfather was one of the leaders of the overthrow, defended its legality in an editorial prepared for Sunday's edition." Lou Cannon, *Waving (and Lowering) Flag in Hawaii Pride*, Wash. Post, Jan. 17, 1993, at A33.

47 Overthrow of Hawaii Resolution, Pub. L. No. 103-150, 1993 U.S.C.C.A.N. (107 Stat.) 1510, 1512.

48 *Id.* ("Presidentially established investigation conducted by Congressmen James Blount into the events surrounding the insurrection and overthrow").

49 *See* Mark A. Inciong, Note, *The Last Trust: Native Hawaiian Beneficiaries Under the Hawaiian Homes Commission Act*, 8 ARIZ. J. INT'L & COMP. L. 174, 191 n. 34 (1991) ("The Blount Report...found that the overthrow... had been illegal...and that Liliuokalani [should] be restored to power").

50 "Whereas, in a message to Congress on December 18, 1893, President Grover Cleveland reported fully and accurately on the illegal acts of the conspirators." Overthrow of Hawaii Resolution, Pub. L. No. 103-150, 1993 U.S.C.C.A.N. (107 Stat.) 1510, 1511.

51 Overthrow of Hawaii Resolution, Pub. L. No. 103-150, 1993 U.S.C.C.A.N. (107 Stat.) 1510, 1511.

52 U.N. CHARTER, art. 1, § 2.

53 Newlands Resolution, Pub. L. No. 55, 30 Stat. 750 (1898).

54 "[I]t was held that, by 1939, the rules on belligerent occupation [that it does not transfer sovereignty] had 'been recognized by all civilized nations and were regarded as being declaratory of the law and customs of war.'" Georg Shwarzenberger, 2 INTERNATIONAL LAW 165 (1965) (citing Nuremburg Judgement, International Military Tribunal, Cmd. 6964 at 65 (1946)).

55 Overthrow of Hawaii Resolution, Pub. L. No. 103-150, 1993 U.S.C.C.A.N. (107 Stat.) 1510.

56 *Id.* at 1512.

57 Mililani B. Trask, *Historical and Contemporary Hawaiian Self-Deter-*

mination: A Native Hawaiian Perspective, 8 ARIZ. J. INT'L COMP. L. 77, 91-95 (1991).

58 "[A]nnexation of occupied territory is a violation of international law... Title to the territory in question must not change until there is either complete subjugation (*debellatio*) or a peace treaty has been put into effect." Gerhard von Glahn, LAW AMONG NATIONS 768 (1992).

59 Overthrow of Hawaii Resolution, Pub. L. No. 103-150, 1993 U.S.C.C.A.N. (107 Stat.) 1510, 1512.

60 Universal Declaration of Human Rights, G.A. Res. 217 (III), U.N. GAOR, 3d Sess., at 71, U.N. Doc A/810 (1948).

61 *Id.* at art. 25.

62 *Id.* at art. 18.

63 Overthrow of Hawaii Resolution, Pub. L. No. 103-150, 1993 U.S.C.C.A.N. (107 Stat.) 1510, 1512.

64 "Belligerent occupation does not transfer sovereignty. Instead it transfers to the occupant the authority to exercise some rights of sovereignty." Von Glahn, *supra* note 58, at 774. *See also* Schwarzenberger, *supra* note 54, at 163-78.

65 Overthrow of Hawaii Resolution, Pub. L. No. 103-150, 1993 U.S.C.C.A.N. (107 Stat.) 1510, 1512.

66 *See* Martin Hession, *The Legal Framework of European Community in International Environmental Agreements*, 2 NEW EUR. L. REV. 59, 103 (Spring 1994).

67 Overthrow of Hawaii Resolution, Pub. L. No. 103-150, 1993 U.S.C.C.A.N. (107 Stat.) 1510, 1512.

68 U.N. CHARTER art. 73.

69 U.N. CHARTER art. 1, ¶ 2.

70 Overthrow of Hawaii Resolution, Pub. L. No. 103-150, 1993 U.S.C.C.A.N. (107 Stat.) 1510, 1512.

71 Convention on the Prevention and Punishment of the Crime of Genocide, Jan. 12, 1951, 78 U.N.T.S. 277.

72 Genocide Convention Implementation Act of 1987, Pub. L. No. 100-106, 102 Stat. 3045 (1987).

73 *See* Case Concerning Application of the Convention on the Prevention and Punishment of The Crime of Genocide (Bosnia & Herzegovina v. Yugoslavia), 1993 I.C.J. 325 (Sept. 13).

74 *See* Francis A. Boyle, The Bosnian People Charge Genocide (1996).

75 Overthrow of Hawaii Resolution, Pub. L. No. 103-150, 1993 U.S.C.C.A.N. (107 Stat.) 1510, 1513.

76 *Id.*

77 Case Concerning the Factory at Chorzow, 1928 P.C.I.J. (ser. A) No. 17, at 1 (Sept. 13).

78 *Id.*

79 Overthrow of Hawaii Resolution, Pub. L. No. 103-150, 1993 U.S.C.C.A.N. (107 Stat.) 1510, 1513.

80 *Id.*

81 *Id.*

82 *Id.*

83 *Id.*

84 U.N. CHARTER art. 1, ¶ 2.

85 Overthrow of Hawaii Resolution, Pub. L. No. 103-150, 1993 U.S.C.C.A.N. (107 Stat.) 1510, 1513.

86 *Id.*

87 *International Covenant on Economic, Social and Cultural Rights*, G.A. Res. 2200 (XXI), U.N. GAOR, 21st Sess., Supp. No. 16 at 49, U.N. Doc. A/6316 (1966).

88 United Nations Convention on the Law of the Sea, opened for signature Dec. 10, 1982, U.N. Doc. A/CONF.62/122, *reprinted in* 21 I.L.M. 1261 (1982).

89 *Universal Declaration of Human Rights*, G.A. Res. 217 (III), U.N. Doc. A/810, at 71 (1948), *reprinted in* 2 DUSAN J. DJONOVICH, UNITED NATIONS RESOLUTIONS (1973).

90 RACIAL DETERMINATION AND THE FEAR OF MISCEGENATION (John D. Smith ed.: 1993).

91 *See* Stephen Kenyer, *Soviet Turmoil: Issue of Citizenship for Ethnic Russians is Dwindling Latvians*, N.Y. TIMES, Sept. 7, 1991, at A1 ("The Lithuanian...authorities are preparing to offer citizenship to all residents who want it").

92 Overthrow of Hawaii Resolution, Pub. L. No. 103-150, 1993 U.S.C.C.A.N. (107 Stat.) 1510.

93 The author served as the legal advisor to the Palestine Liberation Organization on the creation of the Palestinian State from 1987 to 1989.

94 M.K. Gandhi, NON-VIOLENT RESISTANCE (*SATYAGRAHA*) (Schocken ed.: 1971).

CHAPTER 3

KANAKA MAOLI INDEPENDENCE

As related in the previous chapter, during the last week of December 1993 Mr. Kanahele asked me to draft a Declaration of Independence for a Sovereign and Independent Kanaka Maoli Nation State to be issued on the forthcoming anniversary of the illegal overthrow of the Kingdom of Hawaii by the United States on January 16, 1994. I declined the great honor to do this work all by myself on the grounds that since I was not a Kanaka Maoli it would not be appropriate. So an Ohana Council Kupuna and I worked together on this project. It was a joint and collaborative effort, and for Mr. Kanahele and this Kupuna a true labor of love for Hawaii and all Kanaka Maoli.

I took the position that we should not issue a Declaration of Independence on the grounds that the Kingdom of Hawaii was already a sovereign and independent nation state under international law and practice at the time of its illegal overthrow by the United States, which was clearly invalid even in accordance with rudimentary standards of international law in existence at that time. Instead, at my advice we called the instrument a "Proclamation of the Restoration of the Independence of the Sovereign State of Hawaii." We were not "declaring" the "independence" of the Sovereign Kanaka Maoli Nation State. Rather, we were simply "proclaiming" its "restoration."

In my opinion the Kingdom of Hawaii had never been lawfully extinguished in the first place and therefore continued to exist as a state under international law. The Kingdom of Hawaii had been illegally invaded and has been continuously occupied by the U.S. military belligerent occupation forces and a colonial administration regime ever since then. We were simply attempting to restore the "independence" of that former Sovereign Kanaka Maoli Nation State that remained in existence.

The United States was and still is nothing more than the illegal belligerent occupant of the Kingdom of Hawaii with an obligation to evacuate Hawaii immediately. Therefore, we were not seeking to have Hawaii secede from the United States of America either. The United States had illegally invaded and then occupied the Kingdom of Hawaii under the international laws of belligerent occupation starting on January 16, 1893 and continuously from then and on up until today. We simply wanted the United States government to pick up lock, stock, and barrel, and go back home to the Mainland from whence it came and where it belonged. **Yankee go home!**

Finally, we decided to remain neutral concerning the name given to the restored Kanaka Maoli Nation State: "Sovereign Nation State of Hawaii." This was because there existed and still exist reasonable and good faith disagreements about these matters among numerous Kanaka Maoli Sovereignty groups and their respective leaders. We did not wish to offend any of them. Rather, we sought to restore an independent and sovereign Kanaka Maoli Nation State that all Kanaka Maoli could accept and mobilize behind irrespective of their differences.

Moreover, we were in no position to resolve these disputes by ourselves. Pursuant to their right of self-determination, this can only be done among the Kanaka Maoli by themselves in the Spirit of Aloha. We sought to keep all options open for them for the time-being and so as not to alienate any Kanaka Maoli. This Proclamation of Restoration of the Independence of the Sovereign Nation State of Hawaii was intended to be in the name of all Kanaka Maoli.[1] It was written from the Heart. And the Heart of the Kanaka Maoli is Hawaiian, not haole English. The authentic official version of the Proclamation is in Hawaiian.

PROCLAMATION OF THE RESTORATION OF THE INDEPENDENCE OF THE SOVEREIGN NATION STATE OF HAWAI`I

January 16, 1994

`Iolani Palace
Honolulu, O`ahu, Hawai`i

[Official English Version]

Today, We, the Kanaka Maoli, proclaim our Right of self-determination as a People in accordance with Article 1 (2) of the United Nations Charter, and join the World Community of States as an Independent and Sovereign Nation. We hereby reestablish our Independent and Sovereign Nation of Hawai`i, that was illegally taken from the Kanaka Maoli on January 17, 1893.

By virtue of our Right to self-determination, the Kanaka Maoli claim this Right to freely determine our political status and freely pursue our economic, social and cultural development in accordance with common Article 1 of the International Covenant on Civil and Political Rights and the International Covenant on Economic, Social and Cultural Rights.

We, the Kanaka Maoli, claim our Right for our own ends, to freely control and dispose of our natural wealth and resources, including our lands and our waters, without prejudice to any obligations arising out of international economic cooperation, based upon the principle of mutual benefit and international law.

We, the Kanaka Maoli, claim all our Land, Natural Wealth, Resources, Minerals, and Waters, which have always resided and will always reside within the hands of the Kanaka Maoli, to be ours forever, originally under communal land tenure.

Ka Pae `Aina O Hawai`i (the Hawaiian Archipelago) comprises 132 islands, reefs and shoals, stretching 1,523 miles (2,451 kilometers) southeast to northwest across the Tropic of Cancer between 154 40' to 178 25' W longitude and 18 54' to 28 15' N latitude, consisting approximately of a total land area of 6,425 square miles (16,642 square kilometers), including 1 percent of less than six square miles of land area made up of islands off the shores of the main islands and the Northwestern Hawaiian Islands, from Kure Atoll in the North to Nihoa in the South, also Palmyra Island, Midway and Wake Islands, and all Lands that have resided with the Kanaka Maoli since time immemorial. The Hawaiian Islands form an Archipelago, which extends over a vast area of the Pacific Ocean, possessing a 12 mile Territorial Sea, and the 200 mile Exclusive Economic Zone, in accordance with generally recognized Standards of International Law.

In the Independent and Sovereign Nation of Hawai`i live the Kanaka Maoli. We have resided here forever, from time immemorial. We have displaced no other people. We, the Kanaka

Maoli, are the original inhabitants and occupants of these Islands. We have always been in possession of our Land and are entitled to re-establish our Independent and Sovereign Nation.

The current citizens of the Independent and Sovereign Nation of Hawai`i consist of all those who are descendants of the Kanaka Maoli prior to the arrival of the first westerners in 1778, and those persons, and their descendants who have lived in Hawai`i prior to the illegal overthrow, invasion and occupation of January 17, 1893, in the area which now constitutes the Archipelago of the Independent and Sovereign Nation of Hawai`i.

The Independent and Sovereign Nation of Hawai`i will establish procedures for according citizenship by means of naturalization to all people who are habitual residents of Hawai`i as of today's date.

We, the Kanaka Maoli, fully support and subscribe to all of the Rights of the 1948 Universal Declaration of Human Rights for all of the people living in our Independent and Sovereign Nation of Hawai`i, and hereby adopt these protocols on behalf of the citizens of the Independent and Sovereign Nation of Hawai`i.

The Independent and Sovereign Nation of Hawai`i adheres to the generally recognized principles of International Law, including the terms of the United Nations Charter. We will apply for membership in the United Nations Organization. We will conclude other international treaties and agreements at the appropriate time. In the meantime, we call upon the foreign military occupation forces in the Independent and Sovereign Nation of Hawai`i to withdraw from our Sovereign Territory immediately.

We, the Kanaka Maoli, have maintained our close relationship to the `aina (land) and its natural surroundings, through practices spiritual and holistic in nature and in harmony with natural law. The `aina is sacred to us. It sustains us.

Prior to the first European invasion of 1778, Hawai`i was known to have an unique culture and system of government. Through customs and traditional practices, the Kupuna (Elders), were highly regarded and respected as the Keepers of Wisdom and Knowledge, in a highly organized self-sufficient and sustainable social system, based on a communal land tenure system. The Kupuna were always consulted to maintain order and ho`oponopono.

We, the Kanaka Maoli, today embody within our governmental structure traditional customs and culture of the `Aha Kuka O Na Kupuna (Council of Elders), based on mutual respect, traditional practice, and family order. Their consultation on many decisions is highly regarded as the basis of all authority and principle, as handed down through generations of teachings. The Kanaka Maoli's natural ability and practice of Natural Law, commonly known and exercised, due to our deep spiritual connection to nature, and by the use, application and practice of the Laws of Nature, then as now. We, the Kanaka Maoli, believe that all things have life, be they animate or inanimate, as everything has been derived and created from one Source, the Creator.

We, the Kanaka Maoli, respectfully continue to seek the guidance and consultation of our Kupuna, be it Spiritually, Mentally, Physically, Socially or Politically, in consultation and decisions that affect our lives, to restore and protect the customs and teachings of our culture, language and knowledge from being exploited, desecrated and driven to eventual extinction. For all these reasons, the Kupuna Council will serve as the Provisional Government of the Independent and Sovereign Nation of Hawai`i, to provide measures of development, until such time when the Kanaka Maoli will convene a Constitutional Convention.

Despite the historical injustices and abuse that have documented a dark chapter in the lives of the Kanaka Maoli, so unimaginable to the conscience of humanity and to all human life as a whole, we have come to realize that in the course of these modern times, we could never depart or separate our undying love, our connection, or our sacred ties from the Spirit of this Land, Aloha `Aina, which is the heart and life of all living things, as taught and handed down from the ancient wise ones (Kupuna). We must protect our sacred `aina from such invasion and exploitation, to liberate it from alien destructive forces, and preserve and protect our Cultural Heritage for future generations, from the devastation of extinction.

We, the Kanaka Maoli, have continued to exercise, practice and occupy our lands, despite the continued subjection, domination and exploitation by the forces of the occupying foreign powers, denying us our inalienable rights to self-determination, Independence and Sovereignty. Thus have well recognized principles of International Law been violated. Thus were our national identity, land, resources, Right to Sovereignty over our Territory violated, and a peaceful people overthrown by the invasion of foreign powers, who continue to occupy, exploit and destroy our way of life.

We, the Kanaka Maoli, have united at this very historic and symbolic place, the `Iolani Palace, wherein we remember the last days and tragic moments in our history, that have affected the safety and well-being of our people, to which our beloved Kupuna and Queen Liliuokalani and her commitment to restore the rights of our people, have been stolen. Her dedicated endurance against foreign powers who committed such acts of aggression and force, threats of fear and imprisonment, knowingly in violation of numerous treaties, agreements and principles of international customs and law, has never faltered, for the Love of her people, and those who stood on truth and justice, and shall prevail here, now and forever.

We, the Kanaka Maoli, here today in flesh and in Spirit, share that same commitment. It is the duty and obligation of every Kanaka Maoli, young and old, to stand ready to restore and defend our national rights, territorial integrity and independence, without prejudice, and reject and resist unlawful acts, injustice and complicity, violence and terrorism, against our political independence, and do summarily reject such use of violence and force against the territorial integrity of other peaceful states.

If not for those who have continued the struggle for peace, justice and honor, our beloved who have passed in this life and continue standing in spirit beside us here today.

If not for those who have sacrificed their families and lives, who have desired to go to prison rather than be forced to adhere to unjust principles and acts, and who have gone through the crossroads of temptation.

If not for those of us who have awaited this day, who have considered the facts and evidence of such acts of oppression, subjugation and fear, and the loss of their honor, dignity, pride and esteem.

We, the Kanaka Maoli, have historically been the victims of crimes against humanity and genocide, as defined by the Nuremberg Charter and Genocide Convention.

We, the Kanaka Maoli, have the duty to heal our wounds and

restore our integrity, for many have given their lives for us to be here today, that all Kanaka Maoli can once again determine to protect the future destiny of our children, our children's children and their heritage.

The Independent and Sovereign Nation of Hawai`i proclaims its commitment to the purposes and principles of the United Nations Charter. The Kanaka Maoli have long been recognized as a peaceful, loving Nation, choosing to live in peaceful co-existence with other peaceful Nation States, based on liberty, equality, truth and justice, and for the respect of our undying Spirit of Aloha as well as for the Inalienable Rights of Humanity.

We, the Kanaka Maoli, proclaim that despite continued interference of our rights to self-determination, Rights of Sovereignty and Right of Independence by the foreign occupying powers, we stand this day, in all honor, dignity and respect for this Sacred Land, to restore our Independent and Sovereign Nation of Hawai`i.

We, the Kanaka Maoli, pledge that our commitment will continue, until the illegal occupation ends, the revival of the culture of our Independent and Sovereign Nation of Hawai`i has been fortified, the Aloha Spirit is once again fully restored, and the Spirit of Justice, Freedom and Liberation shall once again bring Peace on Earth for all Humanity.

We call upon our Kanaka Maoli people, and upon all Nations of the World, to unite and act this day, to declare and proclaim our Inalienable Sovereignty of the Nation State of Hawai`i, fully restored and functional, and to arise in the uniting of freedom and dignity in our homeland, which is the homeland of the Kanaka Maoli, now and forever.

Therefore, the Kupuna, in General Council Assembled, by the Authority recognized and vested in the Aha Kuka O Ka Ohana, in the name of the Kanaka Maoli people, to preserve and to forevermore cultivate the Heritage and Culture of the Kanaka Maoli, do solemnly publish, declare and proclaim that the Independent and Sovereign Nation of Hawai`i, is free and absolved from any other political connection with any other Nation State. Those who disregard the Principles and Rule of the Law of Nations, Justice, Integrity, Morality of Character, and Humanity, by force and acts of aggression, now illegally occupy our Territory.

We, the Kanaka Maoli, have therefore concluded that the facts are self-evident, that to continue under any colonial regime would cause the destruction and extinction of our Culture and People. We affirm our commitment to the protection of our Divine Heritage. We, the Kanaka Maoli, mutually agree and pledge Our Lives, Our Fortunes and Our Sacred Honor, in the Spirit of Aloha.

Done this sixteenth day of January, nineteen hundred and ninety-four.

In light of and in reaction to having undertaken these extraordinary steps, Mr. Kanahele asked me to write a letter for circulation to all Kupuna in Hawaii setting forth my advice on how they should proceed from there. My edited letter follows:

February 16, 1994
Professor Francis A. Boyle
University of Illinois
207 Law Building
504 East Pennsylvania Ave.
Champaign, IL 61820
(217) 333-7954

To all Kupunas of Hawai'i:

Aloha! Before I begin, I wish to express my gratitude for the fond memories I had during my last visit to Hawai'i. I appreciate the kindness which you have always shown me.

Now as I understand it, the Kupuna Council is looking into examples of where the Kanaka Maoli can go after the passage of Public Law 103-150. I am writing to propose one possibility for the Native Hawaiian people, that of forming your own Nation-State under the principles of International law. This route has several advantages which I will discuss in greater detail below. As I have mentioned in the past, it is not for me to tell the Native Hawaiian people what to do. I am simply offering a vision of the future for the Kanaka Maoli and the manner by which you can achieve it.

Due to the signing of Public Law 103-150, the Kanaka Maoli have a legal advantage no other Native American people has: recognition by the United States Government that it illegally participated in the overthrow of your lawful government and that its subsequent annexation of your lands was illegal. As a result, the United States has recognized that the Kanaka Maoli still hold sovereign authority over Hawai'i. The question for you is how to execute this lawful sovereign authority.

My suggestion is for the Kanaka Maoli, through the Kupuna Council to form your own government and establish diplomatic relations with the rest of the world. This has several advantages for you. First of all, it allows you to immediately recapture the authority which was stolen by the United States government and begin the administration of your lands in accordance with your own laws. Second, your own nation-state would provide greater protection for your people from the genocidal policies of the United States. For example, the Nazis found it much easier to exterminate the Jews and Gypsies during 1939-1945 than other populations, because these people had no state of their own. Finally, it allows you to determine the destiny of your own people, without the interference you've had in the past. You can decide your own fate, and decide for yourself who your citizens will be.

In regards to forming your state, note you already have three of the four elements necessary to be recognized as a nation-state: (1) a fixed territory – the Hawaiian Archipelago; (2) a distinguishable population – the Kanaka Maoli; and (3) a governing structure – the Kupuna Council. The fourth element, the capacity to enter into international relations, would be part of the development of your government.

As I have said, the sovereignty inheres in the Kanaka Maoli. However, in order to exercise your sovereign rights, the Kanaka Maoli must have some form of government, develop your own political systems, establish diplomatic relations, and eventually obtain membership in the United Nations. The first step in this process has already been taken, with the issuance of the Proclamation of Restoration, on the 16th of January, 1994. The next step is to form a provisional government, which could be accomplished at the Kupuna Council meeting from March 4th to the 6th. The provisional government would basically involve the same communal governing structure which you have always had. What you need is (1) a way to organize your people to govern relations among each other, and (2) the capacity to enter into international relations with foreign powers, and to keep commitments made with these nations. Clearly, the Kupuna system is sufficient for the first prong. Therefore, the Kupuna Council should focus on forming a central authority capable of entering into binding commitments with other nations, which in turn is binding on your people. Once this has been accomplished, it will be possible for the Nation of Hawaii to enter into diplomatic relations with other states.

Following the development of the provisional government, plans should be drawn up for a constitutional convention. At the convention, the Kanaka Maoli can decide on the form and permanent structure of your government. The people could decide this aspect, based on referendum or other means. How your government is fashioned is for your people to decide.

Once a formal, permanent government has been established, the Kanaka Maoli can continue to negotiate with foreign powers and proceed to establish diplomatic relations. In addition, Hawai'i can also petition to become a member of the United Nations, if this is your choice.

I wish to reiterate this is for the Kanaka Maoli to decide. I am suggesting one particular vision of the future, and how you would go about achieving it. I urge those of you who have not already done so to read the Declaration of Restoration of January 16th, 1994, and my speech, "Restoration of the Independent Nation State of Hawai'i," which I gave on December 28, 1993. These will provide greater insights to the proposals I have made here.

Thank you for your consideration.
With Highest Regards,

Francis A. Boyle

Immediately after the meeting of the Kupuna Council from March 4 to 6, 1994 mentioned above, Mr. Kanahele asked me to provide him with my advice on how the Government for the Independent and Sovereign Nation State of Hawaii should be structured. My edited response follows:

MEMORANDUM OF LAW

April 15, 1994
From: Professor Francis A. Boyle
To: Bumpy Kanahele
Subject: Proposed Government Structure for the Independent and Sovereign Nation State of Hawaii

Dear Bumpy:

This Memorandum is intended to reply to your request for me to share with you my opinion on a governmental structure for the Nation State of Hawaii....

1. I wish to start this Memorandum by setting forth the basic operational principle: Namely, that the purpose of the Native Hawaiian Government will be to permit the traditional Native Hawaiian culture and patterns of interaction that existed before the European invasion to revive, strengthen, and ultimately to flourish. In other words, we need to devise a structure of government that is most akin to the manner in which the Native Hawaiian People governed themselves before the advent of the European conquest... The whole reason for the Proclamation of the State was to prevent the extinction of the Native Hawaiian People. Likewise, then, the purpose of the government must be to ensure that the Native Hawaiian People can revivify themselves after one hundred years of a most brutal colonial occupation.

2. Conversely, then, it would be counterproductive for the Native Hawaiian People to adopt a structure of government similar to that of the United States of America and the so-called State of Hawaii. This would simply put the Kanaka Maoli into an American straitjacket that would make it impossible for them to revive, strengthen, and flourish as a separate race of people. Otherwise, what is the point of the entire enterprise of proclaiming independence?

3. From this perspective, it then becomes critical to design the Native Hawaiian Government from the ground up, as opposed to the traditional Western model of going from the top down. In other words, we must design a governmental structure that is closest to the Native Hawaiian People, where

the power flows from the People themselves to the government at all levels.

4. That being said, what I would like to propose is as follows: Namely, that there be organized a Peoples Assembly on each one of the islands of the Hawaiian Archipelago that would have full legislative authority to decide the affairs of all the people living on that island. Any citizen of the Kanaka Maoli State of a certain age living on that island would have the right to participate in this Peoples Assembly. The Kanaka Maoli living on the island would have the right to attend the Peoples Assembly; to debate in the Peoples Assembly; to formally make proposals for adoption by the Peoples Assembly; to vote on these proposals, etc. Whatever laws were adopted by this Peoples Assembly would have full force and legal effect throughout the island concerned.

5. This pattern of popular governance would be replicated on an island-by-island basis throughout the Hawaiian Archipelago. There would be rules and procedures for the periodic convocation of the Peoples Assembly on each island in accordance with traditional practices of the Kanaka Maoli, and with procedures for an emergency convocation of the Peoples Assembly if necessary.

6. In between sessions of the Peoples Assembly on each island, the affairs of the island would be governed by the Kupuna Council for that island. The Kupuna Council would be in charge of implementing the laws adopted by the Peoples Assembly and whatever executive functions that need to be discharged for that island. The members of the Kupuna Council for that island would be elected by the Peoples Assembly for that island.

7. Likewise, the Peoples Assembly in consultation with the Kupuna Council for the island will select the members of the Judiciary for that island. The Members of the Judiciary will function in accordance with the traditional Polynesian dispute settlement mechanisms of conciliation, mediation, arbitration, etc. Generally speaking, Kupunas of high repute, standing, integrity and known for wisdom in the community of that island—whether male or female—would be selected to serve on the island Judiciary. It will *not* be required that these judges have a law degree. Likewise, Native Hawaiians who appear before Members of the Judiciary can either plead the cases themselves in accordance with traditional practices, or else select someone

else to represent them. But once again, it is not required that these Kanaka Maoli lawyers have a formal law degree.

8. The Peoples Assembly on each island will select a certain number of Delegates to attend the Hawaiian Peoples Assembly that will govern the affairs of all the Kanaka Maoli People in the Sovereign Nation State of Hawaii. Each island will be able to select a number of Delegates in accordance with the principle of proportional representation. Each Island Peoples Assembly will provide general instructions to their Delegates as to the appropriate positions to be taken in the Hawaiian Peoples Assembly for the benefit of all the Kanaka Maoli including the people whom they represent.

9. The Hawaiian Peoples Assembly will adopt laws that apply throughout the Nation State of Hawaii. Every attempt will be made to avoid conflicts between all-Hawaiian laws and all-island laws. But in the event of a conflict that cannot be resolved by conciliation or mediation, then the all-Hawaiian laws should prevail.

10. This Hawaiian Peoples Assembly will function in accordance with the traditions and practices of the Kanaka Maoli People. The Hawaiian Peoples Assembly will select a Hawaiian Kupuna Council that will serve as the executive branch of government for the Kanaka Maoli Nation State. Acting in conjunction with each other, the Hawaiian Peoples Assembly and the Hawaiian Kupuna Council will have exclusive authority to deal with matters relating to defense, foreign affairs, international trade and investment, Hawaiian commerce, Hawaiian taxation, banking, education, land, health, environment, tourism, etc. To be sure, however, each island Peoples Assembly will instruct their Delegates to the Hawaiian Peoples Assembly as to where the Hawaiian government should stand on these issues.

11. The all-Hawaiian Government should have a limited list of issues in which it has exclusive authority to act as indicated in the above paragraph. But those authorities not expressly granted to the all-Hawaiian Government reside in the hands of the Kanaka Maoli People, and the island Peoples Assemblies. In this fashion, the Kanaka Maoli People will be effectively governing themselves with respect to most matters that concern them personally on a day-to-day basis.

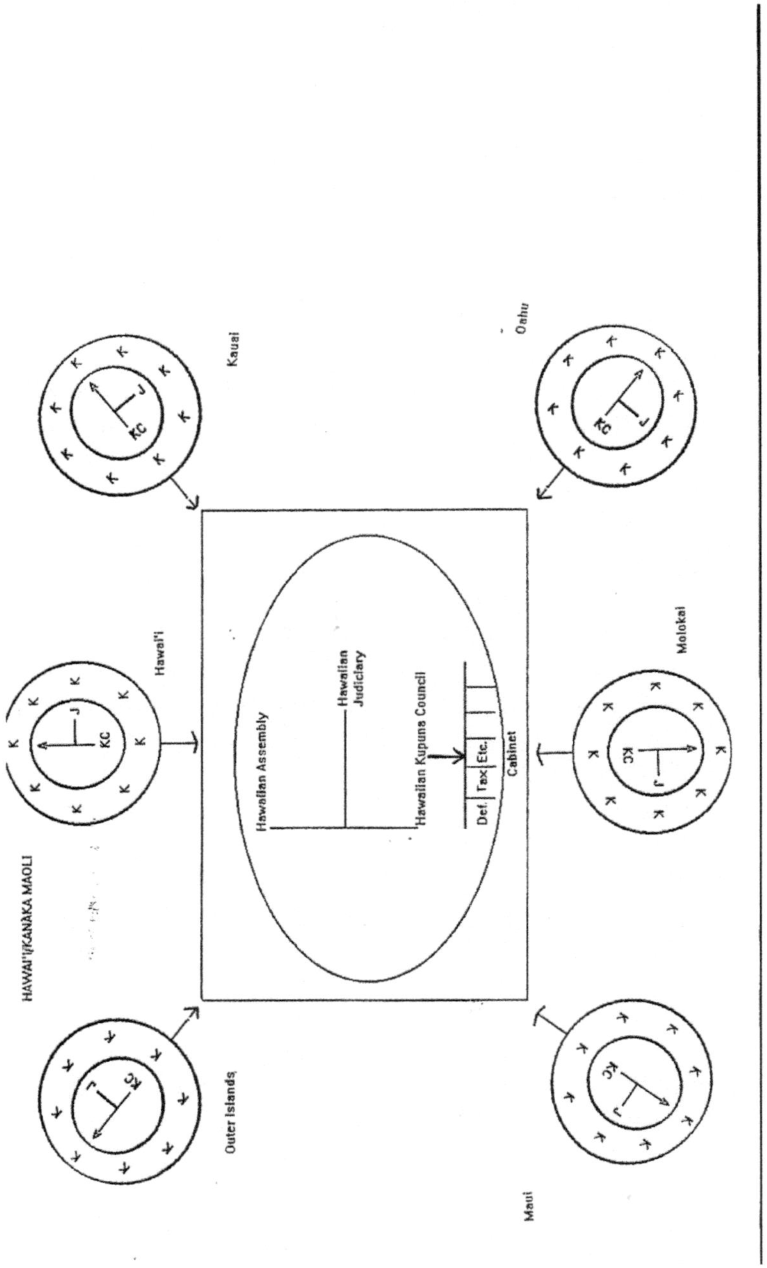

12. The Hawaiian Kupuna Council will select from among

its members the Head of State, Head of Government, and the appropriate Kupunas to discharge the foreign affairs, international trade and investment, commerce, taxation, banking, education, land, health, tourism, the environment, etc. These Kupunas will comprise the Cabinet for the Hawaiian Government.

13. The Hawaiian Peoples Assembly and the Hawaiian Kupuna Council will also select judges for the all-Hawaiian Judiciary. Once again, the task of these judges will be to supervise the laws enacted by the all-Hawaiian Assembly; to interpret and enforce the issues that affect the entirety of the Kanaka Maoli People and the Hawaiian Nation State. Once again, it is not necessary that any of these judges have a law degree from an American or European institution. Likewise, the judges should perform functions of arbitration, mediation, conciliation, and only in the last resort, adjudication. Once again, this would be in accordance with the traditional Polynesian manner of dispute settlement.

14. I think that the above description would constitute a government that would best suit the needs and desires of the Kanaka Maoli People. But of course this is simply a suggestion for you and your Kupunas to consider. In the event there is a general agreement in principle on how to proceed, we can then flesh out the particulars of the proposal later on.

May God be with you and the Kanaka Maoli in your quest for independence.

Best regards,
Yours very truly,

Francis A. Boyle
Professor of International Law

After reviewing my April 15, 1994 Memorandum to him, Mr. Kanahele asked me to draft a proposed Constitution for the Sovereign and Independent Nation State of Hawaii to be considered, debated, revised and approved by their Kupuna Council, which I agreed to do. On this project I worked with my former student, personal research assistant, friend and then General Counsel for the Nation of Hawaii, Mr. Patrick Sickles, Esq. Our deadline was January 16, 1995 in order to commemorate the first Anniversary of the issuance of the Proclamation of Restoration of the Sovereign and Independent Nation State of Hawaii.

After being repeatedly debated and revised by their Kupuna Council, the Constitution was proclaimed at Iolani Palace on January 16, 1995. It was individually signed by 400 Kanaka Maoli including Mr. Kanahele. The Constitution is quite comprehensive. So I am not going to reprint it all here. The full text of the Constitution can be found on the website for the Nation of Hawaii as indicated below. But I am going to reproduce here some of the Constitution's key provisions interspersed with commentaries by me. The text of the Constitution appears in italics. My commentaries follow in regular type. I respectfully offer this Constitution for consideration, debate, revisions, and approval by all Kanaka Maoli.

http://www.hawaii-nation.org/constitution.html

HAWAI'I CONSTITUTION
16 January 1995
Preamble
Aloha Ke Akua

....

Proclamation of Restoration

The Proclamation of Restoration of the Independent and Sovereign Nation-State of Hawai'i of January 16, 1994, is hereby adopted on behalf of the people of the Nation of Hawai'i, and is incorporated into this Constitution with full force and effect as law.

The purpose of this provision is to make it clear that the Proclamation of Restoration has now been fully executed and implemented by the Constitution so that the Proclamation can be relied upon as binding law in any judicial, legislative, or executive proceeding in Hawaii or for any other purpose deemed relevant.

Article II
Enumerated Rights

The people of the Nation of Hawai'i, hereby establish these enumerated rights and equal protections before the law, in all civil and criminal cases, before any court or tribunal heretofore established by this Constitution, or by law. These rights include, but are not limited to, the following:

....

Section 3. Ho'oponopono.

All civil and criminal cases will have automatic access to Ho'oponopono conflict resolution at all times upon consent of all parties.

This provision was included precisely in order to preserve, protect, and promote the traditional Kanaka Maoli dispute settlement procedures based upon dialogue, conciliation, consensus, and reconciliation in the Spirit of Aloha.

Article III
Equal Protection

....

Section 4. Protection against the imposition of the death penalty.

There shall be no death penalty.

Section 5. Protection against unreasonable punishment.

The purpose for the penal laws shall be for the reformation, rehabilitation, and future deterrence of those persons convicted of criminal acts. In no way shall the penal laws of the Nation of Hawai'i be constructed or applied for the purpose of retribution against a person convicted of a criminal act. At no time shall a cruel or unreasonable punishment be applied to a person convicted of a criminal act.

These provisions were included in order to implement the Spirit of Aloha when it comes to dealing with the phenomenon of crime. Hence alleged punishment for the purpose of retribution is strictly prohibited along with the death penalty for any reason.

Chapter II
Structure

Business of the Nation

The Legislative General Assembly of the Nation of Hawai'i

We, the Kanaka Maoli Nationals and Descendants hereby establish this Constitution, and acknowledge that the business of the nation shall be authorized in accordance with this Constitution. All government officials shall comply with this Constitution. All legislative powers shall be vested in a Legislative General Assembly composed of Na Kupuna Council and the Citizens' Assembly. All powers and subjects of legislation shall not be inconsistent with this Constitution.

Here the traditional Kanaka Maoli Kupuna Council is preserved and incorporated as an essential component of the way the Kanaka Maoli govern themselves under the Constitution.

Article VI
The Citizens' Assembly

The Citizens' Assembly shall consist of Representatives elected by the qualified voters from the Districts in which the Representatives reside.

Section 1. Composition

The Citizens' Assembly shall be comprised of 112 representatives, 56 Nationals and 56 Citizens. Every Island shall elect their own representatives to the Citizens' Assembly as follows:

a. 14 Island of Hawai'i
b. 14 Island of Maui
c. 14 Island of Moloka'i
d. 14 Island of O'ahu
e. 14 Island of Kaua'i
f. 14 Island of Lana'i (to be held in trust until there is representation)
g. 14 Island of Kaho'olawe (to be held in trust until there is representation)
h. 14 Island of Ni'ihau (to be held in trust until there is representation)

Notice that representation in the Citizens' Assembly is organized on an island-by-island basis. This is the way the Kanaka Maoli traditionally organize themselves. And beneath that level of organization the Kanaka Maoli organize themselves on an ohana-by-ohana basis. Hence Sovereignty flows from the ground on up around the entire archipelago of Hawaii and in the Spirit of Aloha.

Article VII
Na Kupuna Council

There shall hereby be established a Na Kupuna Council consisting of

Kanaka Maoli Nationals. Na Kupuna Council shall be elected to sit in Council for a specified term of office.

Section 1. Composition.

Na Kupuna Council shall be comprised of 56 Members. Every Island shall elect their own members to Na Kupuna to sit in the Legislative General Assembly as follows:

a. 7 from the Island of Hawai'i
b. 7 from the Islands of Maui
c. 7 from the Islands of Moloka'i
d. 7 from the Island of O'ahu
e. 7 from the Islands of Kaua'i
f. 7 from Kaho'olawe (to be held in trust until there is representation)
g. 7 from Ni'ihau (to be held in trust until there is representation)
h. 7 from Lana'i (to be held in trust until there is representation)

....

Section 4. Qualifications for Office.

All Kupuna shall be eligible for this office who are acknowledged and recognized ('ike) by their peers as teachers of the culture, and each Island shall determine the qualifications of its Kupuna. Kupuna shall be no less than 45 years of age.

The traditional Kanaka Maoli governing mechanism of the Kupuna Council is preserved and incorporated into the overall structure of government. Once again, it is organized on an island-by-island basis which is how the Kanaka Maoli traditionally organize themselves. And beneath that level of organization the Kanaka Maoli organize themselves on an ohana-by-ohana basis. Thus, Sovereignty flows from the ground on up around the entire archipelago of Hawaii and in the Spirit of Aloha.

Executive Powers
The Executive Administration

There shall be established an Executive Administration, which shall consist of the Head of State, a Deputy Head of State, and all Ministries established for the purposes of executing the laws and the business of the Nation.

This language was deliberately kept neutral so that the Kanaka Maoli could someday select a Head of State who is a King or a Queen; or a constitutional monarch; or a democratically elected monarch; or a president; or a prime minister; or a chief or a chieftess; or any other office that they mutually agree upon in the Spirit of Aloha. The term "Head of State" was specifically designed to transcend for the time-being the reasonable and good faith disagreements that the Kanaka Maoli have among themselves on these matters.

Judiciary

Article X
The National Tribunals

The National Tribunals are hereby established to exercise solely all judicial authority and functions as established by this Constitution. The Judicial Power shall be vested in one Supreme Tribunal, and in such inferior tribunals as the Legislative General Assembly deems necessary and proper to establish. The Tribunals shall have original and appellate jurisdictions, or as the Citizens' Assembly shall provide by law.

....

Section 5. Qualifications of Judges.

Every judge shall be a Kanaka Maoli National, and use common sense to justify fairness, compassion, firmness and honesty in customary Hawaiian law and the laws of this Constitution.

The customary laws of the Kanaka Maoli are expressly preserved and incorporated into the Constitution as a source of law to be applied by all judges in the Spirit of Aloha.

Article XII
Administrative Laws

....

Section 4. Enforcement.

All citizens have a right to enforce the Constitution, Treaties, and laws of the Nation in any court or Tribunal having jurisdiction.

This provision is in there to make it clear that imperious judges have no authority to interpret out of meaningful existence the Constitution and its incorporated Proclamation together with Treaties when relied upon in court by the citizens of the Kanaka Maoli Nation State.

Article XIII
Home Rule
Section 1. Definitions.

a. .Home Rule is defined as those powers not specifically of a National character relating to Island or local government. Home Rule allows each Island to administer its own affairs without interference from the National Government.

b. Island Administration.
Each Island shall create an administration for those affairs which are the exclusive purview of the Island.

Section 2. Administration.

Domestic responsibilities of each Island are those powers not specifically reserved to the National government in this Constitution. Each Island shall be responsible for allocating powers of the Island government.

Section 3. Island Administration.

Each Island shall be responsible for setting up its own administration, which shall be of the same democratic form as the National government. Each Island government shall be independent from any other, and no Island shall be responsible for the actions of another Island.

Section 4. Limitation.

There shall be no laws or regulations inconsistent with this constitution.

The Kanaka Maoli organize themselves on an ohana-by-ohana basis and then on top of that on an island-by-island basis. I have seen this unique system of self-governance myself in operation during my many lectures throughout the Hawaiian Islands. These provisions on Home Rule are specifically intended to preserve and protect and promote the resurgence of this traditional Kanaka Maoli manner of governing themselves in the Spirit of Aloha.

Article XV Citizenship
Section 1. Citizenship.

a. Kanaka Maoli National

b. A Kanaka Maoli is defined as any person who by birth or national origin and ancestry is a descendant of the original inhabitants who prior to 1778 exercised sovereignty over the Archipelago of Hawai'i.

c. Citizens, Naturalized.

The Legislative General Assembly shall provide by law a naturalization process for all persons who qualify and choose to become citizens of the Nation.

These provisions on Citizenship go back to the proposals I suggested in my 1993 Mable Smyth Hall Address. Notice the Constitution says nothing at all about the infamous genocidal, racist and deliberately divisive "blood-quantums" established and enforced by the United States government against American Indians. In the Spirit of Aloha, a law will be adopted whereby non-Kanaka-Maoli can petition to become naturalized citizens of Hawaii if they so desire. It could be possible to arrange this so that U.S. citizens resident in Hawaii would not forfeit their U.S. citizenship when they become naturalized citizens of Hawaii. A green-card system could also be established so that current non-Kanaka-Maoli residents of Hawaii can remain as permanent resident aliens without becoming naturalized citizens of Hawaii.

In the Spirit of Aloha, the Kanaka Maoli have no intention or desire to deport non-Kanaka-Maoli from Hawaii. Rather, the Kanaka-Maoli seek to create a "win-win" solution and situation for themselves and all non-Kanaka-Maoli currently resident in Hawaii. It is that desire and the Spirit of Aloha that animate and underlie this entire Constitution.

Article XVI
Laws Pertaining to Lands and Cultural Preservation
Section 1. National lands of the Kanaka Maoli Nationals.

Prior to 1778, the Kanaka Maoli Nationals lived in a communal land tenure system, and every National had the right and privilege to receive and acquire the use of land.

Section 2. Transition to communal land tenure.

Na Kupuna shall provide laws for a transitional system of land use for all its Nationals and Citizens.

Section 3. Communal land tenure.

No person or group of persons, or entity or groups of entities, may own or dispose of National land, all National land being held in trust for the Kanaka Maoli Nationals by this government. A person may apply for the usage of these lands, consistent with the requirements of law.

Section 4. Claims of the Kanaka Maoli Nationals.

All national lands and resources heretofore lawfully claimed by the Kanaka Maoli Nationals are held in absolute common undivided interest held in perpetuity for the Kanaka Maoli Nationals forever.

Each and every speck of Hawaii was brutally stolen by the United States in the American rape of Hawaii. Therefore, everyone who believes that he, she, or it have legal title to land in Hawaii is mistaken and deceived. The United States is nothing more than the illegal belligerent occupant of Hawaii and is thus obligated to administer Hawaii under the international laws of belligerent occupation, which it has never done. Thereunder, the U.S. belligerent occupant holds the land and natural resources of Hawaii in trust for the Kanaka Maoli who are its true owners. Belligerent occupants do not have title to land. Therefore belligerent occupants cannot transfer valid title to land to anyone.

Furthermore, the U.S. belligerent occupant is under an obligation to prevent colonial settlers from its Homeland from moving into territory that it occupies in Hawaii and stealing land from the original inhabitants, the Kanaka Maoli. Today, the transfer of settlers into occupied territory by a belligerent occupant is an internationally recognized war crime and a crime against humanity. In the case of the Kanaka Maoli, it is also an element of the genocide that the United States government has historically inflicted upon them since 1893.

Title to all land in Hawaii is vested in the Kanaka Maoli themselves; and on a communal basis; and not as individuals. Therefore individual Kanaka Maoli cannot be tempted by non-Kanaka-Maoli to sell off any parcels of land that have been allocated to them for their beneficial use and enjoyment. The land in Hawaii can never again be alienated from the Kanaka Maoli. As a matter of fact, the land in Hawaii was never lawfully alienated from the Kanaka Maoli in the first place.

All those who think they have a fee simple absolute title to any land in Hawaii are dead wrong. Those bogus and defective claims will not be respected. However, transitional arrangements will be instituted to facilitate these new realities. For example, it could be possible to convert a bogus fee simple absolute title to land into a lawful 99-year leasehold upon the payment of rent to the Kanaka Maoli government for the benefit of the Kanaka Maoli. Non-Kanaka-Maoli could remain in possession of the Kanaka Maoli land that they now illegally occupy but only as lawful leaseholders. So instead of paying off a mortgage to a bank, non-Kanaka-Maoli will be paying rent to the Kanaka Maoli government. The price could be calculated to remain about the same. These 99-year leaseholds could also be bought and sold on a free market system, thus permitting non-Kanaka-Maoli to leave Hawaii if that is what they plan to do. But current leaseholders would have to be citizens or lawful residents of Hawaii in accordance with Kanaka Maoli laws. No rentier class of absentee non-Kanaka-Maoli leaseholders would be permitted.

There is not space here to detail all the ramifications of these provisions. But they have been carefully thought through by everyone involved in the drafting and approval of this Constitution. These matters of land tenure will all be handled by the Kanaka Maoli in accordance with the Spirit of Aloha in order to accommodate non-Kanaka-Maoli to the maximum extent feasible consistent with the fundamental interests of the Kanaka Maoli in preserving, protecting, and reviving their Independent Nation State after all the genocide that has been perpetrated upon them by the United States government and by non-Kanaka-Maoli. Once again, we are dealing with the innocent victims of 121+ years of American genocide, crimes against humanity, war crimes, and apartheid. Steps must be taken to revive the Kanaka Maoli language, culture, religion, customs, traditions, and heritage so that the Kanaka Maoli can flourish once again. The non-Kanaka-Maoli's mistaken and unreasonable expectations about their bogus and defective property claims must be subordinated to the resurgence of the Kanaka Maoli's way of life. That being said, based upon all the work I have done with them since 1992, I submit that the Kanaka Maoli are willing to work out all these matters with non-Kanaka-Maoli in good faith and in the Spirit of Aloha.

Article XVII
Transitional Provisions
Section 1. Corporate Entities.

Upon the ratification of this Constitution, any illegal entity, corporate or otherwise, shall not be immediately dissolved. The Nation of Hawai'i shall provide sufficient notice to these entities and their responsible officers, agents, owners, or otherwise. Time shall be granted to allow these entities to state their claims and desire to function under the Nation of Hawai'i.

Section 2. Accountability.

All illegal occupying governmental agencies of the State of Hawai'i, the United States of America, corporate entities, foreign governments and individuals shall be responsible and accountable for the actions of their agents and officials in any criminal or civil claims under either this Constitution or international customary, conventional or criminal law.

Section 3. Requirement for treaty.

Any settlement of claims between the Nation of Hawai'i and the United States of America can only be resolved by a Treaty which has been accepted in accordance with this Constitution.

Section 4. No limitations for remedies.

This Constitution, and any laws hereunder enacted, shall not limit the lawful government hereby constituted from seeking any other remedy provided by law.

Section 5. Governmental transition.

The illegal occupying foreign regime of the State of Hawai'i and the United States of America may continue to provide services in Hawai'i to such extent necessary as the government of the Nation of Hawai'i shall deem proper and expedient for a peaceful transition towards restoration.

Section 6. Repeal of inconsistent legislation.

Upon the ratification of this Constitution, all laws of the State of Hawai'i and the United States of America inconsistent with this Constitution are hereby repealed and have no force and effect.

Ratification

Done in Convention by the Unanimous Consent of na Kanaka Maoli present at `Iolani Palace, Honolulu, O`ahu o Hawai`i Nei this Sixteenth Day of January in the Year of Our Lord one thousand nine hundred and ninety five for the Independence of our Nation in Witness whereof We hereunto place our names,

In the Spirit of Aloha, the Kanaka Maoli will bend over backwards to keep those non-Kanaka-Maoli currently living in Hawaii as residents or citizens of their Kanaka Maoli Nation State. The Kanaka Maoli will not do to non-Kanaka-Maoli what the United States government and the non-Kanaka-Maoli have done to them! As the ultimate victims of American genocide, war crimes, crimes against humanity, and apartheid the Kanaka Maoli fully subscribe to that hallowed principle of "Never again!"

That is what the Kanaka Maoli Spirit of Aloha is all about. Not Western-style vengeance. But Polynesian reconciliation. The Kanaka Maoli hand of friendship is extended to all non-Kanaka-Maoli in the Spirit of Aloha. This Constitution proves it. This Constitution is that Kanaka Maoli hand of friendship offered to non-Kanaka-Maoli in the Spirit of Aloha. I respectfully recommend that non-Kanaka-Maoli accept it and embrace this Constitution.

ENDNOTES

1 Jon Yoshishige, *Group Declares Hawaiian Independence*, Honolulu Advertiser, Jan. 17, 1994.

CHAPTER 4

THE HAWAIIAN KINGDOM AT THE UNITED STATES SUPREME COURT

In early 1998 the Regent for the Hawaiian Kingdom, Mr. Keanu Sai, asked me to give him my advice on what steps I believed he could take at the United States Supreme Court in order to restore the Hawaiian Kingdom so as to reverse the illegal annexation of Hawaii by the United States for the upcoming 100th anniversary. I recommended to Mr. Sai that we file a Bill of Complaint against the United States on behalf of the Hawaiian Kingdom before the United States Supreme Court towards the end of restoring the Hawaiian Kingdom on the basis of the so-called Original Jurisdiction Clause of the United States Constitution set forth in Article III, Section 2 thereof that gives the U.S. Supreme Court original jurisdiction in "all Cases affecting Ambassadors, other public Ministers and Consuls":

> In all Cases affecting Ambassadors, other public Ministers and Consuls, and those in which a State shall be Party, the Supreme Court shall have original Jurisdiction.

In other words, we could file a lawsuit on behalf of the Hawaiian Kingdom against the United States directly with the United States Supreme Court without having to proceed through two levels of intermediate Federal courts. Furthermore, in accordance with its jurisprudence, for the purpose of these proceedings the United States Supreme Court would be sitting as an international court administering and applying international law.

Since I was admitted to practice law before the U.S. Supreme Court, I agreed to serve as Counsel to the Hawaiian Kingdom and its Regent, Mr. Sai, on these proceedings. Mr. Sai and I further agreed that I would perform the legal research, writing, and argumentation for this lawsuit, while he would be in charge of the factual submissions. But this was truly a joint and collaborative effort by Mr. Sai and me on behalf of the Hawaiian Kingdom and the Kanaka Maoli. For Mr. Sai this Supreme Court lawsuit in order to restore the Hawaiian Kingdom upon the 100th anniversary of its illegal annexation by the United States was a true Labor of Love and in the Spirit of Aloha.

Mr. Sai personally filed our lawsuit with the Clerk of the United States Supreme Court in Washington, D.C. on August 6, 1998, on or about the 100th anniversary of the illegal annexation of Hawaii by the United States. We captioned our lawsuit *The Hawaiian Kingdom and David Keanu Sai, Regent of the Hawaiian Kingdom and Ambassador of the Hawaiian Kingdom to the United States, Plaintiffs v. The United States of America and William Jefferson Clinton, President of the United States of America, Defendants.* As filed the lawsuit consisted of four documents: (1) Motion for Leave to File a Bill of Complaint; (2) the Complaint itself; (3) a Memorandum in Support thereof; and (4) an Appendix thereto. I have reprinted below only the Motion and the Complaint. The Memorandum in support thereof and the Appendix thereto are omitted because they repeat the basic facts in great detail of the illegal overthrow of the Hawaiian Kingdom by the United States government that have already been essentially discussed and analyzed above in chapter 2 of this book.

When such a lawsuit is filed the usual practice is for the Clerk of the Court to cash the check for the filing fee, docket the case on the Court's schedule, issue a docket number to the Plaintiffs, and transmit a copy of the docketed documents to the Defendants. Pursuant to their earlier precedents, I had anticipated that the Justices of the U.S. Supreme Court would soon thereafter summarily dismiss our lawsuit without any oral or written submissions by me as Counsel by means of an Order without a written opinion. Most astonishingly, that is not what happened.

Instead, the Clerk of the United States Supreme Court returned our original filed documents to Mr. Sai undocketed, together with his uncashed check for the filing fee. What happened here is explained in the third document reprinted below that we entitled Motion to Direct the Clerk of the Court to File a Motion for Leave to File a Bill of Complaint, Complaint, and Memorandum in Support, dated October 8, 1998, that was filed with the Clerk of the U.S. Supreme Court with a check for the filing fee. This new Motion was docketed by the Clerk of the Court and the check for the filing fee was cashed. On November 2, 1998, the U.S Supreme Court denied this new Motion without a written opinion as follows:

> David Keanu Sai, et al., v. United States, et al.
> No. M-26
> Supreme Court of the United States
> Nov. 2, 1998
> The motion to direct the Clerk to file a motion for leave to file a bill of complaint is denied.
> 119 S.Ct. 398 (Mem.), 1998 WL 758884 (U.S., Nov. 2, 1998)

At the very beginning of my recommending these Supreme Court proceedings to Mr. Sai, that Order was the outcome I had expected to occur right after the filing of our original Motion and Bill of Complaint on August 6, 1998. What happened?

The basic procedural facts behind these two Supreme Court Motions of August 6, 1998 and October 8, 1998 are recounted below in the second Motion of October 8. So I am not going to repeat them all here. But to make a long story short: Upon receipt of the returned undocketed documents and the uncashed check, Mr. Sai had a lengthy discussion with Mr. Francis J. Lorson, the Deputy Clerk of the U.S. Supreme Court. Not getting anywhere with Mr. Lorson, Mr. Sai informed him that he was going to have me call him about this matter because I was serving as Counsel to the Hawaiian Kingdom and Mr. Sai on the case, and that I was admitted to practice law before the U.S. Supreme Court. So I called Mr. Lorson and conducted a 45-minute long conversation with him that covered all aspects of this litigation. I am not going to recapitulate the substance of that 45-minute conversation here. But the material facts surrounding the original filing of our Motion and Complaint on August 6, 1998 as explained to me by Mr. Lorson were as follows:

Upon the filing of our documents, the Justices of the United States Supreme Court ordered their Clerk to contact the U.S. Department of State and ask them if the United States government recognized the Hawaiian Kingdom. The State Department informed the Clerk that the United States government did not recognize the Hawaiian Kingdom. The Clerk duly reported this information to the Justices of the U.S. Supreme Court. The Justices then met twice more for a sum-total of three meetings on our August 6 Motion and Complaint. Whereupon the Justices of the United States Supreme Court ordered the Clerk to return the papers undocketed to Mr. Sai together with the check for the filing fee uncashed.

As far as I could figure out from my 45-minute conversation with the Deputy Clerk Mr. Lorson, after three meetings on our August 6 Motion and Complaint, the Justices of the United States Supreme Court ultimately decided to apply the constitutional law doctrine of "unrecognized foreign sovereigns" to the Hawaiian Kingdom. Pursuant thereto, foreign sovereign nation states that are not diplomatically recognized by the United States government are denied all access to United States Courts—as if they did not exist either legally or factually.[1] Accordingly, our documents were never docketed, our check for the filing was never cashed, and everything was returned to Mr. Sai by the Clerk.

In other words, in 1998 the Justices of the United States Supreme Court had treated the Hawaiian Kingdom as if it were a full-fledged foreign sovereign nation state that was not diplomatically recognized by the United States government. This Supreme-Court-ordered and constitutional-law-mandated shut-out of the Hawaiian Kingdom from U.S. courts was similar to the treatment given to the Union of Soviet Socialist Republics from its foundation in 1917 by means of the Bolshevik Revolution until its official recognition by the Franklin Roosevelt administration in 1933 when the U.S.S.R. had likewise been excluded from U.S. courts for the exact same reason.[2] **Breathtaking!**

> August 6, 1998
> Dear Friends:
>
> I just received a phone call from Keanu Sai in Washington D.C. He has just filed the lawsuit against the United States government and President Clinton at the U.S. Supreme Court on behalf of the Hawaiian Kingdom, demanding restoration of the Kingdom and reparations for all harm inflicted, to be held in trust for the Native Hawaiian People. He will hold a Press Conference tomorrow (Friday) morning at 10 am Washington time on the steps of the Supreme Court. CNN will be there, along with NBC, ABC, and CBS. Keanu will attend the Aloha march to commemorate the 100th anniversary of the non-annexation of the Hawaiian Kingdom, and then return to Hawaii for the celebrations there at the Palace next week. Of course, Keanu will have to speak for himself. But I have prepared a little statement of my own:

Although I cannot be here today because of a previous commitment, I stand in proud support of Keanu Sai and this historically important lawsuit that he and the Office of the Regent of the Hawaiian Kingdom are starting against the United States government in order to restore the Hawaiian Kingdom. One hundred five years ago, the Hawaiian Kingdom was stolen by a group of American citizens acting with the illegal support of the United States government. Thieves cannot obtain or convey valid title to anything. As this lawsuit will establish, the United States never lawfully acquired the Hawaiian Kingdom. Despite 105 years of aggression, colonialism, military occupation, and genocide, the Hawaiian Kingdom still exists. It is up to each and every one of us to do whatever we can in our own way and in accordance with our own talents to restore the Hawaiian Kingdom as an Independent Nation State, and with full-fledged Membership in the United Nations Organization.

Aloha.

Francis A. Boyle.

Professor of International Law

The following two documents were filed with the United States Supreme Court on behalf of the Hawaiian Kingdom against the United States on August 6, 1998.

MOTION

In the
Supreme Court of the United States
October Term, 1998

No. 98-_______

The Hawaiian Kingdom, and
David Keanu Sai, Regent of the Hawaiian Kingdom and Ambassador of the Hawaiian Kingdom to the United States, Plaintiffs,

v.

The United States of America, and
William Jefferson Clinton, President of the United States of America.

Defendants
Original Action

Motion for Leave to File a Bill of Complaint

Plaintiffs the Hawaiian Kingdom and David Keanu Sai, as Regent of the Hawaiian Kingdom and as Ambassador of the Hawaiian Kingdom to the United States, respectfully move this Court for leave to file a Bill of Complaint and Memorandum in Support in an original action, pursuant to 28 U.S.C. § 1251(b)(1), for reasons more fully set forth therein.

In conjunction with this Motion, Plaintiffs file a Complaint and a Memorandum in support of this Motion.
Dated: August 4th, 1998

Respectfully submitted,

David Keanu Sai
Regent of the Hawaiian Kingdom and Ambassador of the Hawaiian Kingdom to the United States
P.O. Box 2194
Honolulu, Hawai'i 96805-2194
(808) 239-5347

COMPLAINT

In the
Supreme Court of the United States
October Term, 1998

No. 98-_______

The Hawaiian Kingdom, and
David Keanu Sai, Regent of the Hawaiian Kingdom and Ambassador of the Hawaiian Kingdom to the United States, Plaintiffs,

v.

The United States of America, and
William Jefferson Clinton, President of the United States of America.

Defendants
Original Action

COMPLAINT

This action is brought by Plaintiffs Hawaiian Kingdom and David Keanu Sai, as Regent of the Hawaiian Kingdom and as Ambassador of the Hawaiian Kingdom to the United States, to enforce and give effect to (1) the Treaty of Friendship, Commerce, and Navigation of December 20, 1849 between the United States and His Majesty King Kamehameha III, the King of the Hawaiian Islands, 18 Stat. 406; (2) the Convention on Commercial Reciprocity of January 30, 1875 between the United States and His Majesty Kalākaua, the King of the Hawaiian Islands, 19 Stat. 625, at 69; (3) the December 6, 1884 Supplementary Convention to the 1875 Commercial Reciprocity Convention, between the United States and the Hawaiian Kingdom, 25 Stat. 1399; (4) the Apology Law, Pub. Law 103-150, 103d Cong. (1993); and (5) principles of customary international law related thereto. A permanent injunction is necessary to prevent Defendants from violating Plaintiffs' rights under these Treaties and Laws as well as under customary international law. In addition, Plaintiffs seek reparations for all harm inflicted upon them and the Subjects of the Hawaiian Kingdom, the Native Hawaiian People, for violation of these Treaties, Laws and customary international law, to be held in trust by the Plaintiffs for the benefit of the Native Hawaiian People. Finally, Plaintiffs respectfully request this Court to order the relief of *restitutio in integrum* for the Hawaiian Kingdom.

NATURE OF THE ACTION

1. Plaintiffs bring this action for declaratory relief that the Defendants have violated their rights under the 1849 Treaty of Friendship, Commerce and Navigation, the 1875 Convention on Commercial Reciprocity, the 1884 Supplementary Convention, the 1993 Apology Law and principles of customary international law.

2. In addition, Plaintiffs bring this action for permanent injunctive relief preventing Defendants from violating their rights under these international Treaties, Federal Laws, and principles

of customary international law.

3. In addition, Plaintiffs seek reparations for all harm inflicted upon them and the Subjects of the Hawaiian Kingdom, the Native Hawaiian People, for violation of their rights under these international Treaties and Federal Laws and customary international law, to be held in trust by the Plaintiffs for the benefit of the Native Hawaiian People.

4. In addition, Plaintiffs seek the relief of *restitutio in integrum* for the Hawaiian Kingdom.

JURISDICTION

5. This is a case "affecting Ambassadors, other public Ministers and Consuls" within the original jurisdiction of the United States Supreme Court under article III, section 2 of the United States Constitution as well as under 28 U.S.C. § 1251(b)(1).

6. In addition, this is also a case "arising under this Constitution, the Laws of the United States, and Treaties made, or which shall be made, under their Authority" under article III, section 2 of the United States Constitution.

THE PARTIES

7. Plaintiff Hawaiian Kingdom is a foreign state.

8. Plaintiff David Keanu Sai is a Subject of the Hawaiian Kingdom, Regent of the Hawaiian Kingdom, and also Ambassador of the Hawaiian Kingdom to the United States.

9. Plaintiff David Keanu Sai brings this action in his capacities as a Public Minister of the Hawaiian Kingdom and as Ambassador of the Hawaiian Kingdom to the United States on behalf of the Hawaiian Kingdom and its Subjects, the Native Hawaiian People, including himself.

10. Defendant United States of America has treaty relations with the Hawaiian Kingdom and thus obligations thereunder and under customary international law towards Plaintiffs and the Subjects of the Hawaiian Kingdom, the Native Hawaiian People.

11. Defendant William Jefferson Clinton is President of the United States of America. Pursuant to article II, section 3 of the United States Constitution, the President "shall take Care that the Laws be faithfully executed." That responsibility, by virtue of Article VI of the United States Constitution, extends to treaties signed by the United States and ratified by the United States Senate.

FACTS

12. On December 20, 1849, a Treaty of Friendship, Commerce, and Navigation, between the United States of America and His Majesty King Kamehameha III, the King of the Hawaiian Islands, was concluded and signed at Washington. Ratifications by both countries were exchanged at Honolulu, island of O'ahu, on August 24, 1850, and the treaty was in force from that date, for the term of ten years, and further until either of the contracting parties shall give notice to the other of its intention to terminate. Article I of the Treaty of 1849, provides that there *"...shall be perpetual peace and amity between the United States and the King of the Hawaiian Islands, his heirs and his successors."* (emphasis added). Furthermore, Article VIII of the treaty provides that "...each of the two contracting parties engages that the citizens or subjects of the other residing in their respective States shall enjoy their property and personal security in as full and ample manner as their own citizens or subjects, or the subjects or citizens of the most favored nation, *but subject always to the laws and statutes of the two countries, respectively."* (emphasis added). In addition, article XVI provides that any *"citizen or subject of either party infringing the articles of this treaty shall be held responsible for the same, and the harmony and good correspondence between the two governments shall not be interrupted thereby, each party engaging in no way to protect the offender, or sanction such violation."* (emphasis added). Neither country gave notice to the other of its intention to terminate this treaty in accordance with article XVI of the said treaty. Therefore the treaty is still in full force and legal effect until today and at all times relevant to these proceedings. This treaty is part of the "supreme Law of the Land" under Article VI of the United States Constitution.

13. On January 30, 1875, a Convention on the subject of Commercial Reciprocity between the United States of America and His Majesty Kalăkaua, the King of the Hawaiian Islands, was concluded and signed at Washington. Ratifications by both countries were exchanged at Washington on June 3, 1875, and the treaty was in force from that date, for the term of seven years, and further until either of the contracting parties shall give notice to the other of its intention to terminate. Neither party ever expressed their intention to terminate. The Convention proclaims that the "...United States of America and His Majesty the King of the Hawaiian Islands, equally animated by the desire to strengthen and perpetuate the friendly relations which have heretofore uniformly existed between them, and to consolidate their commercial intercourse, have resolved to enter into a Convention for Commercial Reciprocity." This treaty is still in full force and legal effect until today and at all times relevant to these proceedings. This treaty is part of the "supreme Law of the Land" under Article VI of the United States Constitution.

14. On December 6, 1884, a Supplementary Convention to this 1875 Commercial Reciprocity Convention between the United States of America and the Hawaiian Kingdom was signed at Washington. On November 9, 1887, ratifications were exchanged and the Convention was to extend for a term of seven years from that date, and further, until the expiration of twelve months after either of the high contracting parties shall give notice to the other of its wish to terminate the same. This Supplementary Convention provided the exclusive right of the United States government "...to enter the harbor of Pearl River in the Island of O'ahu, and to establish and maintain there a coaling and repair station for the use of vessels of the United States...." Neither party to the Supplementary Convention of 1884 ever gave notice to the other of its intent to terminate the same in accordance with said convention's terms. This treaty is still in full force and legal effect until today and at all times relevant to these proceedings. This treaty is part of the "supreme Law of the Land" under Article VI of the United States Constitution.

15. The United States Naval facilities subsequently established at Pearl Harbor materially exceeded the grant of authority set out in article II of the said Convention of 1884.

16. On the afternoon of January 17, 1893, a self-declared "committee of safety" [consisting of haoles] that represented the American and European sugar planters, descendants of missionaries, and financiers, including and primarily Citizens of the United States, committed the crime of high treason as defined under § 1, Chapter VI of the Hawaiian Penal Code, by deposing Her Majesty Queen Lili'uokalani and her cabinet and proclaimed the establishment of a provisional government, until terms of annexation with the United States of America have been negotiated and agreed upon. A United States diplomat assigned to the Hawaiian Kingdom, namely Minister John L. Stevens, conspired with these traitors and authorized U.S. troops to land on Hawaiian soil against the protest of Queen Lili'uokalani and her cabinet, under the false pretense that American lives were in jeopardy.

17. On that same day, when informed of the risk of bloodshed with resistance, Her Majesty Queen Lili'uokalani issued a statement "temporarily" yielding her executive authority as the constitutional Monarch to the United States Government, by its President, [to function] as a fact finder only, rather than to the provisional government.

18. In violation of the treaties cited above and principles of customary international law, the United States Minister Stevens extended diplomatic recognition to the provisional government, that was formed by these traitors, including and primarily Citizens of the United States, without the consent of the Government of the Hawaiian Kingdom, while United States Marines forced and imposed themselves upon and across the Government building. Thereafter, all Government employees were forced to sign oaths of allegiance to the provisional government, or risk termination of their employment.

19. On January 19, 1893, individuals representing the self-declared provisional government sailed for the United States in a steamer especially chartered for the occasion, and arrived in San Francisco on January 28th, and in Washington on February 3rd. On February 14, 1893, they signed a treaty of annexation with the United States' Secretary of State, who was operating on the mistaken assumption that it was a popular revolt and

no troops or officers of the United States were present or took any part whatever in the uprising. On February 15, 1893, the treaty of annexation was submitted to the United States Senate for ratification. Upon receipt of the Queen's Protest, President Cleveland withdrew from the Senate the treaty of annexation, and dispatched a representative to Hawai'i to impartially investigate the causes of the so-called revolution and to report the same.

20. The official report of a Presidentially established investigation conducted by former U.S. Congressman James Blount into the events surrounding the treasonous actions and overthrow of January 17, 1893, concluded that the United States diplomatic and military representatives had abused their authority and were responsible for the overthrow of the Hawaiian Kingdom Government. App. II, Foreign Relations of the U.S. 1894, 53d Congress. 3d sess., House of Rep., Ex. Doc. 1, part 1, Affairs in Hawai'i. Defendants are bound by the contents of the said Blount Report for the purpose of these proceedings.

21. On the basis in part of the Blount Report, in a Message to Congress on December 18, 1893, President Grover Cleveland reported fully and accurately on the illegal acts of these traitors, described such acts as an "act of war, committed with the participation of a diplomatic representative of the United States and without authority of Congress," and acknowledged that by such acts the government of a peaceful and friendly people was overthrown. He reminded the United States Congress of the special conditions of Queen Lili'uokalani's surrender of Hawai'i's sovereignty, where she "...surrendered not to the provisional government, but to the United States. She surrendered not absolutely and permanently, but temporarily and conditionally until such time as the facts could be considered by the United States." House Executive Documents No. 47, 2nd Sess. 53rd Cong. 1893-94, Vol. 27; "Hawaiian Islands," pp. iii-xvi. Defendants are bound by President Cleveland's Message to Congress for the purpose of these proceedings.

22. President Cleveland further stated that a "substantial wrong has thus been done which a due regard for our national character as well as the rights of the injured people requires we

should endeavor to repair" and called for the restoration of the Government of the Hawaiian Kingdom. He also stated "...that the United States could not, under the circumstances disclosed, annex the islands without justly incurring the imputation of acquiring them by unjustifiable methods, I shall not again submit the treaty of annexation to the Senate for its consideration, and in the instructions to Minister Willis, a copy of which accompanies this message, I have directed him to so inform the provisional government."

23. On July 4, 1894, the provisional government declared itself to be the Republic of Hawai'i, and maintained their opposition to the restoration of the Hawaiian Kingdom Government as called for by United States President Grover Cleveland.

24. On June 16, 1897, a second attempt of a treaty of annexation was signed in Washington, D.C., between representatives of the self-proclaimed Republic of Hawai'i and the newly elected President of the United States of America, William McKinley, but said treaty remained subject to ratification by the United States Senate. This treaty was never ratified.

25. On June 17, 1897, in Washington, D.C., Her Majesty Queen Lili'uokalani filed in the State Department of the United States, a formal protest to the treaty of annexation that attempted to transfer the territory and sovereignty of the Hawaiian Kingdom to the United States of America.

26. Fortifying Her Majesty Queen Lili'uokalani's second letter of protest were signature petitions of 38,554 Hawaiian subjects and residents of the Hawaiian Kingdom from the organizations of the Hawaiian Patriotic League and the Hawaiian Political Party, who vehemently protested annexation and whose petitions were filed in the Senate of the United States of America previous to its convening in December of 1897 and in the U.S. State Department. These signatures represented ninety-five percent (95%) of the Native Hawaiian population at that time. As a result of the aforesaid protests the United States Senate failed to obtain the required 2/3's vote, as mandated by the United States Constitution, to ratify the treaty of annexation with the self-proclaimed Republic of Hawai'i. The United States

of America never lawfully acquired the Hawaiian Kingdom.

27. On November 3, 1993, the United States Congress enacted Public Law 103-150, 103d Congress, (hereinafter referred to as the "Apology Law.") that acknowledged the 100th anniversary of the January 17, 1893 illegal overthrow of the Hawaiian Kingdom Government, and offered an apology to Native Hawaiians. The Defendants are bound by this so-called Apology Law for the purpose of these proceedings. The Defendants have done nothing to implement the terms of the 1993 Apology Law.

COUNT ONE

(Continuing Violation of the 1849 Treaty of Friendship, Commerce and Navigation)

28. Plaintiffs repeat and reallege paragraphs 1 through 27.

29. Defendants, their employees, officers, agents, their predecessors and their successors, have continuously violated the 1849 Treaty of Friendship, Commerce and Navigation between the United States and the Hawaiian Kingdom from January 17, 1893 until today.

COUNT TWO

(Continuing Violation of the 1875 Commercial Reciprocity Convention)

30. Plaintiffs repeat and reallege paragraphs 1 through 29.

31. Defendants, their employees, officers, agents, their predecessors and their successors, have continuously violated the 1875 Commercial Reciprocity Convention between the United States and the Hawaiian Kingdom from January 17, 1893 until today.

COUNT THREE

(Continuing Violation of the 1884 Supplementary Convention)

32. Plaintiffs repeat and reallege paragraphs 1 through 31.

33. Defendants, their employees, officers, agents, their predecessors and their successors, have continuously violated the 1884 Supplementary Convention between the United States and the Hawaiian Kingdom from January 17, 1893 until today.

COUNT FOUR

(Continuing Violation of 1993 Apology Law)

34. Plaintiffs repeat and reallege paragraphs 1 through 33.

35. Defendants, their employees, officers, agents, their predecessors and their successors, have continuously violated the 1993 Apology Law from its effective date until today.

COUNT FIVE

(Continuing Violation of Customary International Law)

36. Plaintiffs repeat and reallege paragraphs 1 through 35.

37. Defendants, their employees, officers, agents, their predecessors and their successors, have continuously violated principles of customary international law with respect to the Hawaiian Kingdom and its Subjects, the Native Hawaiian People, from January 17,1893 until today.

PRAYER FOR RELIEF

WHEREFORE, Plaintiffs respectfully request:

A. That a decree be entered adjudging and declaring that the Defendants have violated the 1849 Treaty of Friendship, Commerce and Navigation, the 1875 Commercial Reciprocity Convention, the 1884 Supplementary Convention, the 1993 Apology Law, and principles of customary international law related to the Hawaiian Kingdom and its Subjects, the Native Hawaiian People.

B. That a decree be entered perpetually enjoining the Defendants, their employees, officers, agents and successors from violating the 1849 Treaty of Friendship, Commerce and Navigation, the 1875 Commercial Reciprocity Convention, the

1884 Supplementary Convention, the 1993 Apology Law, and principles of customary international law related to the Hawaiian Kingdom and its Subjects, the Native Hawaiian People.

C. That a decree be entered ordering the Defendants to pay reparations for their violations of the 1849 Treaty of Friendship, Commerce and Navigation, the 1875 Commercial Reciprocity Convention, the 1884 Supplementary Convention, the 1993 Apology Law, and principles of customary international law related to the Hawaiian Kingdom and its Subjects, the Native Hawaiian People, to be held in trust by the Plaintiffs for the benefit of the Native Hawaiian People.

D. That a decree be entered ordering *restitutio in integrum* for the Hawaiian Kingdom.

E. For such other and further relief that this Court may deem proper and necessary.

Dated: August 4th, 1998

Respectfully submitted,
David Keanu Sai
Regent of the Hawaiian Kingdom and Ambassador
of the Hawaiian Kingdom to the United States
P.O. Box 2194
Honolulu, Hawai'i 96805-2194
(808) 239-5347

The following Motion was filed in the United States Supreme Court on behalf of the Hawaiian Kingdom against the United States on or about October 8, 1898.

In the Supreme Court of the United States
October Term, 1998
No. 98-_______

The Hawaiian Kingdom, and David Keanu Sai, Regent of the Hawaiian Kingdom and Ambassador of the Hawaiian Kingdom to the United States, Plaintiffs, v.

The United States of America, and
William Jefferson Clinton, President of the United States of America.
Defendants
Original Action

Motion to Direct the Clerk of the Court to File a Motion for Leave to File a Bill of Complaint, Complaint and Memorandum in Support

Plaintiffs the Hawaiian Kingdom and David Keanu Sai, as Regent of the Hawaiian Kingdom and as Ambassador of the Hawaiian Kingdom to the United States, respectfully move this Court to direct the Clerk of the Court to file a Motion for Leave to File a Bill of Complaint, Complaint, and Memorandum in Support in an original action, pursuant to 28 U.S.C. § 1251(b)(1) and Article III, § 2 of the United States Constitution, for reasons more fully set forth herein. In conjunction with this Motion, Plaintiffs re-file a Motion for Leave to File a Bill of Complaint, Complaint, and a Memorandum in Support, together with an Appendix thereto.

Plaintiff David Keanu Sai is a Native Hawaiian Subject and resident of the Hawaiian Kingdom and requests to enter the original jurisdiction of the United States Supreme Court under Article III, §2 of the United States Constitution and under 28 U.S.C. 1251(b)(1) on the grounds that Plaintiff David Keanu Sai is the Ambassador of the Hawaiian Kingdom to the United States in addition to being a Public Minister of a foreign country. Plaintiff David Keanu Sai is appointed Regent of the Hawaiian Kingdom, pro tempore, under and by virtue of the Hawaiian Kingdom Constitution of 1864, and herein serves as its Ambassador to the United States of America.

The President of the United States, as an official charged by law, "...shall take care that the laws be faithfully executed...," U.S. Constitution, Article II, §3,; "...and all Treaties made, or which shall be made, under the Authority of the United States, shall be the supreme Law of the Land..." Id., Article VI, §2.

In these proceedings, the United States Supreme Court sits as an International Court administering the law of nations, that is international law, including treaties and customary international law. Plaintiff David Keanu Sai is here to present these claims for the first time in 105 years since the illegal overthrow of the Hawaiian Kingdom, and 100 years since the purported and illegal annexation of the territory of the Hawaiian Kingdom by the United States in violation of the 1849 Treaty of Friendship, Commerce and Navigation, the 1875 Commercial Reciprocity Convention, the 1884 Supplementary Convention, and basic principles of customary international law pertaining to the Hawaiian Kingdom and its Subjects, the Native Hawaiian People.

On August 6, 1998, a Motion for Leave to file a Bill of Complaint, Complaint, Memorandum in Support and Appendix thereto were hand delivered to the Clerk of the United States Supreme Court to be filed under the Court's original jurisdiction by Plaintiff David Keanu Sai, as appointed Regent of the Hawaiian Kingdom, pro tempore, and serving in the capacity of Ambassador of the Hawaiian Kingdom to the United States of America, on the basis of Article III, §2 of the United States Constitution, and 28 U.S.C. §1251(b)(1), against the United States of America and William Jefferson Clinton, President of the United States, to enforce the rights of the Hawaiian Kingdom and its Subjects under the treaties entered between the Hawaiian Kingdom and the United States, the law of nations, and customary international law.

Plaintiffs hereby incorporate by reference this Motion for Leave to File a Bill of Complaint, Complaint and Memorandum in Support, and Appendix thereto. Original copies of Plaintiffs' Pleadings are attached to this Motion. Plaintiffs hereby repeat, reaffirm, reallege and renew the entire contents of Plaintiffs' Motion for Leave to File a Bill of Complaint, Complaint and Memorandum in Support and Appendix thereto in this instant Motion to Compel the Clerk to File Plaintiffs' original Pleadings. Plaintiffs' original Pleadings are hereby re-filed as an integral part of this Motion.

On August 12, 1998, the Clerk of the Supreme Court, William K. Suter, by Francis J. Lorson, notified Plaintiff by correspondence that the "...motion for leave to file a bill of complaint and appendix were received August 6, 1998, and must be returned." The Clerk cited that Plaintiff David Keanu Sai was not an attorney admitted to the Bar of the United States Supreme Court, and therefore Plaintiff Sai could not represent anyone other than himself. The Clerk further stated that this Court does not have original jurisdiction over a complaint filed by the Hawaiian Kingdom and that Plaintiff Sai is not an Ambassador. Pursuant to the rules set forth by this Court, a Clerk does not have the authority to question the face of the complaint nor the moving party, this being reserved to the Defendants and/or the Justices of the Court.

Furthermore, in international courts and proceedings it is common for the Ambassador to represent the State. Therefore, as its Ambassador, Plaintiff Sai certainly has the right to represent the Hawaiian Kingdom.

On August 27, 1998, Plaintiff Sai spoke on the telephone to Francis J. Lorson, Deputy Clerk, in an attempt to understand why the Complaint was returned. In response to the letter of correspondence dated August 12, 1998, Plaintiff Sai asserted that the statements alleged are not for the Clerk of the Court to decide, but rather for the Solicitor General in the brief in opposition. The Clerk answered that he did have the authority to deny the Complaint, but when Plaintiff Sai stated "...tell me which rule of the Supreme Court gives the authority for the Clerk to determine the content of the case aside from its specifications of size and dimensions." He said Rule 1.1. Plaintiff Sai responded that "...Rule 1.1 mentions nothing about content. The content is reserved for the Defendant to answer and not the Clerk." In conclusion, Francis J. Lorson stated that "...if you are questioning my authority you can file a Motion to Direct the Clerk of the Court to file the Motion for Leave to File a Bill of Complaint. The Justices will look at the Motion and they'll make a decision."

Francis J. Lorson also told Plaintiff Sai that if he were to place the Complaint on the docket it would open the floodgate for all types of complaints. Plaintiffs assert that the legal rights of Native Hawaiians and the Hawaiian Kingdom have never been adjudicated by the Court and that under the U.S. Constitution and federal law Native Hawaiians are not treated in the same respect as Native Americans. Therefore United States court decisions over Native Americans cannot be construed to be applicable to Native Hawaiians and the Hawaiian Kingdom. This is a case of first impression.

Thereafter Plaintiff Sai requested Professor Francis A. Boyle, legal advisor to the Hawaiian Kingdom and the office of Regent, to speak with Francis J. Lorson, Deputy Clerk, to assure him that the complaint and Plaintiff Sai's capacity as Regent of the Hawaiian Kingdom and Ambassador were filed in good faith and therefore the case should be placed on the docket under the Court's original jurisdiction. Professor Francis A. Boyle is an Attorney-at-Law in good standing before the Bar of the United States Supreme Court and has practiced law before the International Court of Justice in The Hague. **When Professor Boyle expressed his opinion that both the Rules and the precedents were sufficiently flexible to permit the docketing of Plaintiffs' original Pleadings, Mr. Lorson conceded that he was acting pursuant to verbal instructions issued to him by the Justices of the Court.**

With all due respect, Plaintiffs are compelled to request the Justices of the United States Supreme Court to execute all official duties in accordance with the principles, ethics, honor and rules of this esteemed Court.

Your Honors know that it is with great remorse when I say it is somewhat disheartening when the highest court in America suggests its inability to discern politics from law. The actions of the United States Supreme Court regarding the filing of the abovementioned Complaint, infers much more than a suspicion, I fear it is a clear and present danger which compromises the proper administration of justice. I say this mainly because the principal belief amongst most Native Hawaiians is their unquestioning faith in the law, and I can only pray that the recent actions of your Court do not discourage them from that faith.

One must confess that in examining the records and opinions of some of the historical arguments which this Honorable Court has settled, one cannot help but to admire in the words of this Court and former Courts, the mark of great propriety and admirable judgment throughout its history, which one must acknowledge has served to raise the character and integrity of the highest American judicial authority for justice and moderation. Your Honors, on behalf of the Hawaiian Kingdom and its People, and in the sacred name of justice, I appeal to your sense of propriety, and ask that this Honorable Court afford Plaintiffs all the courtesies, rights and privileges accorded Plaintiffs under international law.

I am compelled to share this thought as I am convinced it is a true representation of our People's sentiments. It is not now, nor has it ever been the Hawaiian Kingdom's intent to call international attention to *our* (Hawaii vs. U.S.) peculiar predicament. For the most part, we remain optimistic, dare I say confident that this unfortunate episode in both our histories can be resolved in an amicable and civilized manner, so as to avoid incident in most regards. That is our desire. However, I cannot emphasize enough the predicament all interested parties will be put in if this information should be sprung upon the world's communities without warning. How this revelation transpires into cause and effect is now in your hands, and I am hopeful that some positive and productive activity in regards to the betterment and advancement of both our Peoples shall be forthcoming.

On December 19, 1893, in a message to the United States Congress, President Grover Cleveland, representing the highest office of the Executive branch of government, determined that the overthrow of the Government of the Hawaiian Kingdom was predicated and dependent upon the unauthorized and illegal use of United States diplomatic and military power. One hundred years later, on November 23, 1993, the Legislative branch of the United States Government passed a joint resolution acknowledging that the overthrow of the Hawaiian Kingdom Government was "illegal" and offered an apology to the Native Hawaiian People. And now one hundred years since the purported annexation of the Hawaiian Islands on August 12, 1898, by a joint resolution and not a treaty of annexation, the issue is now being presented to the third and final branch of the United States government, being the Judicial branch, its Supreme Court.

The fundamental rights which we assert, being liberty, freedom, and independence, and which by right is ours to claim, are the same rights which you as free people fought and died for against a former oppressor, and that which most of your citizenry still regard as your nation's greatest prize.

As I ponder the duty of the United States Supreme Court, I cannot help but to recall the words of the great American John Quincy Adams who lamented; "I can never join with my voice in the toast which I see in the papers attributed to one of our gallant naval heroes. I cannot ask of heaven success, even for my country, in a cause where she should be in the wrong. *Fiat justitia, pereat coelum*. My toast would be, may our country be always successful, but whether successful or otherwise, always right."

For the foregoing reasons, Plaintiffs respectfully request that this Court (1) grant Plaintiffs' Motion to Direct the Clerk of the Court to file Motion for Leave to File a Bill of Complaint, Complaint, Memorandum in Support and Appendix thereto, (2) grant leave requested in Plaintiff's Motion for Leave to file a Bill of Complaint, and (3) grant relief requested in Plaintiffs' Bill of Complaint.

Dated: October 8, 1998

Respectfully submitted,

Regent of the Hawaiian Kingdom and
Ambassador of the Hawaiian Kingdom
to the United States

P.O. Box 2194
Honolulu, Hawaii 96805-2194

(808) 239-5347

ENDNOTES

1 American Law Institute, 1 Restatement of the Law Third: The Foreign Relations Law of the United States § 205 (1987).

2 *Id*. at Reporters' Note 1.

CHAPTER 5

THE KANAKA MAOLI REJECT KANAKAMAOLI-LANDUSTAN

By means of Section 1(3) of the 1993 Apology Resolution, the American Congress made an "ACKNOWLEDGEMENT... of the rights of Native Hawaiians to self-determination." According to international law and practice, this right to self-determination must include the option of establishing an independent state if that is the desire of the Kanaka Maoli as freely expressed. In regard to this latter point, the 1993 Apology Resolution also stated quite clearly that: "Whereas, the indigenous Hawaiian people never directly relinquished their claims to their inherent sovereignty as a people or over their national lands to the United States, either through their monarchy or through a plebiscite or referendum..." The obvious implication of this language is that the American Congress believes that the Kanaka Maoli have a right to "a plebiscite or referendum" whereby they can exercise "their inherent sovereignty as a people or over their national lands," including their "rights of Native Hawaiians to self-determination," which means an independent state if that is their desire as freely expressed by means of "a plebiscite or referendum."

Furthermore, the 1993 Apology Resolution sets forth the following disclaimer at the very end of the law: "Nothing in this Joint Resolution is intended to serve as a settlement of any claims against the United States." The obvious implication of this language is that the American Congress recognizes that the Kanaka Maoli have valid "claims against the United States," including "their claims to their inherent sovereignty as a people or over their national lands" as well as their "rights of Native Hawaiians to self-determination," which means an independent state if that is their desire as freely expressed by means of "a plebiscite or referendum."

As fully explained in chapter 2 of this book, the ramifications of the numerous acknowledgements, admissions, and concessions by the American Congress in the 1993 Apology Resolution are truly cosmic. Someday there will have to be a final settlement of all claims by the Kanaka Maoli against the American government—especially their land claims—by means of their exercise of their right to self-determination, which could mean establishing an independent state if that is their desire as freely expressed by means of a legitimate plebiscite or referendum. In other words, the current political and economic situation of the American state of Hawaii is invalid, unstable, and precarious because it is without legal foundation. By means of the 1993 Apology Resolution the American Congress itself pulled the proverbial rug out from under their self-styled 50th state of the American "Union" as well as all purported legal title to land ownership in the illegal American state of Hawaii.

This uncertainty has already created a serious economic problem for Hawaii. At the bottom of the mountain, a capitalist economy is founded upon people and legal entities possessing valid title to land that can be freely transferred to others as well as upon the owners' ability to take out loans that are secured on the basis of that valid title to land. In a capitalist economic system, without certainty of valid title to the land upon which it sits, the economy will progressively slow down and eventually grind to a halt. This is because without valid title to land, the transaction risks and thus costs of all economic activities are increased, passed along, and multiplied. The entire economy of Hawaii has become a House of Cards tottering perilously on a beach of dry white sand.

So after the 1993 Apology Resolution the American plutocrats illegally in charge of the illegally-created American state of Hawaii realized that they were somehow going to have to settle the Kanaka Maoli land claims to all of Hawaii and thereby "quiet title" to them—as the Anglo-American Law of Real Property quaintly phrases it. In other words, they needed to eliminate as a matter of law the Kanaka Maoli claims to all the land in and natural resources of Hawaii. Hence the American plutocrats presently illegally in possession must and necessarily will strive to "settle" the claims of the Kanaka Maoli and "quiet title" to all their land claims in Hawaii in order to protect their own economic self-interests and moreover to further enrich themselves into the indefinite future at the expense of and to the grave and fatal detriment of the Native Hawaiians.

In order to convince the Kanaka Maoli to surrender all of their claims under international law as recognized by the 1993 Apology Resolution—including therein independence, sovereignty, self-determination, their lands, their natural resources, genocide, reparations, etc. as discussed in the preceding chapters of this book—the American plutocrats, their illegal American state of Hawaii, and the illegal belligerent occupant of Hawaii known as the United States Federal Government and Congress would in return most graciously endow the Kanaka Maoli with a bogus "sovereignty" along the lines of an Indian Reservation or of a Bantustan for Blacks in the former apartheid South Africa. There the Kanaka Maoli might have some minor degree of fake autonomy where they could build casino complexes located within tourist resorts organized along the lines of Disneyworld but with Kanaka-Maoli-theme-parks and access to the pristine pure beaches of Hawaii. I have derisively referred to this grotesque and obscene illegal American vision for the future of the Kanaka Maoli as Kanakamaolilandustan.

It would be like Sun City in the apartheid Bantustan of Bophuthatswana—a.k.a. "Boph," which no longer exists in apartheid-free South Africa. Kanakamaolilandustan would bring with it gambling, casinos, organized crime, prostitution, drugs, liquor, pornography, junk bonds, odious debt, etc. Kanakamaolilandustan would constitute the ultimate debasement and final degradation of the Kanaka Maoli. This is the illegal American occupiers' "final solution" to what they perceive to be their inconvenient Kanaka Maoli "problem."

Notice that the illegal American occupiers are trying to inflict upon the Kanaka Maoli what the Afrikaners inflicted upon the Blacks of South Africa: apartheid. Apartheid is a crime against humanity in accordance with article 1 of the 1973 Apartheid Convention and article 7(1)(j) of the 1998 Rome Statute of the International Criminal Court. And also what the United States of America has inflicted upon the Indians: genocide. Genocide is the most reprehensible international crime of all under the 1948 Genocide Convention to which the United States is a contracting party. Chapter 1 of this book has already established that the United States government has inflicted genocide against the Kanaka Maoli from 1893 continuously up until today.

Kanakamaolilandustan has been designed to finish off the Kanaka Maoli for good: extinction. Why would the United States Government treat the Kanaka Maoli any better than or any differently from the genocidal manner in which America has exterminated numerous Indian Nations and Peoples and Languages? Conversely, why would the Kanaka Maoli want to tread down the same one-way path toward extinction of so many American Indian Nations and Peoples who have already disappeared upon from the pages of history and from the ranks of humanity?

The American plutocrats, the illegal American state of Hawaii, and the illegal belligerent occupant of Hawaii known as the U.S. Federal Government and Congress are smart and devious enough to realize that in order to legitimate Kanakamaolilandustan in the eyes of the world, they must somehow obtain the apparent "consent" of the Kanaka Maoli to their own enserfment, enslavement, and final extinction. This would be accomplished by means of a fraudulent "plebiscite or referendum" to which the American Congress had already implicitly determined the Kanaka Maoli are entitled in their 1993 Apology Resolution, but that would nevertheless be completely and illegally controlled and dominated by the Americans in order to produce this lucrative but genocidal predetermined end-result of Kanakamaolilandustan for the Kanaka Maoli. The first attempt to perpetrate this extinctual swindle against the Kanaka Maoli was made by the illegal American state of Hawaii. Soon after the Proclamation of the Restoration of Independence of the Sovereign State of Hawaii on January 16, 1994, and in direct reaction thereto, the illegal American state of Hawaii proceeded to establish a process calling for a Kanaka Maoli "plebiscite" for the purpose of convening a "Constitutional Convention" that would create a Native Hawaiian "nation" that would all be under the total control and domination of the illegal Americans from the get-go.

Intuitively smelling a rat, Mr. Kanahele asked me to study the parameters of this illegal American-state-imposed "plebiscite" upon the Kanaka Maoli, and to provide him with an Opinion Letter on it for circulation to all Kanaka Maoli. I fulfilled his request by means of a 9 March 1995 Opinion Letter reprinted below that sets forth the requirements for a true "plebiscite" under international law and practice whereby the Kanaka Maoli would be able to engage in a legitimate exercise of their right to self-determination under international law and practice, including establishing an independent state of their own if that is their desire as freely expressed. On the basis of my 9 March 1995 Opinion Letter, Mr. Kanahele, the Nation of Hawaii, and many other Sovereignty leaders and groups organized popular resistance all over Hawaii among the Kanaka Maoli and their supporters against this bogus "plebiscite." As a result thereof, its name was changed from "plebiscite" to "vote."

Because of the extended and impersonal process of transmission of communications from Champaign, Illinois, U.S.A. to Hawaii, there then developed some confusion among Kanaka Maoli Sovereignty groups and their leaders over whether I now supported the "vote" after its name had been changed from "plebiscite." In an effort to clarify the situation I then issued a second Opinion Letter dated April 5, 1996 for circulation to all Kanaka Maoli opposing the "vote" because it still did not fulfill the requirements for a valid "plebiscite" under international law and practice. I have reprinted below my two Opinion Letters so that the Kanaka Maoli and their supporters will know exactly what the requirements are for a real "plebiscite or referendum" whereby the Kanaka Maoli can validly exercise their rights to self-determination and inherent sovereignty, including establishing an independent state of their own if that is their desire as freely expressed thereby.

Because of the monumental economic and political factors briefly discussed above, these issues are not going away. The illegal American state of Hawaii and the illegal belligerent occupying power of Hawaii known as the U.S. Federal Government and Congress will continue to concoct new schemes in order to rob the Kanaka Maoli of their lands, their natural resources, their inherent sovereignty, their right to self-determination, etc. Forewarned is forearmed! Forearmed is forewarned! These two Opinion Letters are intended to forewarn and to forearm the Kanaka Maoli and their supporters the next time the illegal American state of Hawaii and/or the illegal belligerent occupant of Hawaii known as the U.S. Federal Government and Congress predictably attempt to perpetrate yet another existential bait-and-switch operation upon the Native Hawaiians.

When it was clear that the illegal American state of Hawaii could not bring forth Kanakamaolilandustan, the illegal belligerent occupying power in Hawaii known as the United States Federal Government and its Congress then took their stab at finishing off the Kanaka Maoli and all of their claims under international law as recognized by the 1993 Apology Resolution. This was done by means of the so-called Akaka Bill, introduced into the American Congress by Senator Daniel Akaka representing the illegal American state of Hawaii: S.344, 108th Congress, 1st Session (February 11, 2003). There was also a companion piece of legislation introduced into the American House of Representatives by American Congressman Neil Abercrombie representing the illegal American state of Hawaii: H.R. 665, 108th Congress, 1st Session (February 11, 2003). There were some important material differences between these two versions of Kanakamaolilandustan that will be commented upon below.

Sensing an existential threat, Mr. Kanahele—acting on behalf of the Nation of Hawaii—and the official Office of Hawaiian Affairs invited me to go on a lecture tour around the Hawaiian Islands in late December of 2004 in order to sound the klaxon against the Akaka Bill and in addition to explain an alternative means for securing the Restoration of Hawaii's Independence instead of the Akaka/Abercrombie versions of

Kanakamaolilandustan. Reprinted below is the transcribed and edited text of one of these public lectures that I delivered in Honolulu on December 29, 2004 against the Akaka Bill at the official request of the Office of Hawaiian Affairs and the Nation of Hawaii. It was then submitted by Mr. Kanahele on behalf of the Nation of Hawaii to American Senator John McCain, Chair of the American U.S. Senate Indian Affairs Committee in opposition to the then current version of the Akaka Bill that was to be the subject of Hearings by that American Committee on March 1, 2005, as well as to all the Members of the American United States Senate.

The Akaka legislation together with its later variants and successors eventually died in the American Congress for a variety of reasons, including and especially because of strident opposition mounted by the Kanaka Maoli themselves and their supporters. Nevertheless undaunted, American plutocrats from the illegal American state of Hawaii persisted with pursuing their perverted vision of establishing Kanakamaolilandustan up to and including American Congressman Neil Abercrombie's Native Hawaiian Government Reorganization Act of 2009, H.R. 2314, 111th Congress, 2d Session (2010)—all to no avail. In 2010 American Congressman Abercrombie then left the American House of Representatives in order to become the illegal American colonial administrative "Governor" of the illegal American state of Hawaii. But because of the enormous economic incentives at stake and perverse political motivations arising therefrom, a successor to the Akaka/Abercrombie legislation and its grotesque and obscene and genocidal vision of Kanakamaolilandustan is certain to be revived repeatedly by both the illegal belligerent occupant of Hawaii known as the United States Federal Government and its Congress as well as by the illegal American State of Hawaii and by the illegal American plutocrats.

Kanakamaolilandustan is like a vampire. You have to put a stake through its heart in order to kill it off once and for all. This chapter constitutes that stake driven through the heart of Kanakamaolilandustan. Death to Kanakamaolilandustan! **Free Hawaii!**

WHY A "PLEBISCITE"?

The Sovereignty Elections Council and the so-called Plebiscite on Hawaiian Sovereignty

On March 18, 1995, Head of State of the Nation of Hawai`i Pu`uhonua Kanahele presented to the Hawai`i Sovereignty Elections

Council (HSEC) the official opinion of Professor of International Law Dr. Francis Anthony Boyle, regarding the requirements for a "plebiscite" according to generally recognized standards of international law and practice. (see text of letter below) The question must be asked, Why call it a "plebiscite"? The intended process is clearly not a plebiscite, and using the term only causes fear and confusion among the people of Hawai`i regarding this important issue and process, recalling the illegal 1959 "plebiscite" by which statehood was imposed on Hawai`i. (see UN Charter, Article 73)

The Nation of Hawai`i supports the efforts of the Council towards education and unification, under Article XVII "Transitional Provisions" of the Hawai`i Constitution of 16 Jan. 1995 (Section 5. Governmental transition. The illegal occupying foreign regime of the State of Hawai`i and the United States of America may continue to provide services in Hawai`i to such extent necessary as the government of the Nation of Hawai`i shall deem proper and expedient for a peaceful transition towards restoration).

However, the Nation will withdraw its support if the needed change is not made to eliminate the word "plebiscite."

Letter Concerning the Requirements for a Plebiscite

University of Illinois at Urbana-Champaign College of Law
204 Law Building
504 East Pennsylvania Avenue
Champaign, IL 61820
217 333-0931
217 244-1478 fax

March 9, 1995

The Honorable Pu`uhonua Kanahele
Head of State
Hawai`i
Post Office Box 80
Waimanalo, O`ahu, Hawai`i

Dear Sir,

You have asked me to render an opinion on whether or not the elections to be supervised by the Hawaiian Sovereignty Elections Council as described in H.B.976 would constitute a genuine "plebiscite" in accordance with the generally recognized standards of international law and practice. At a minimum, international law and practice would require the following conditions to be fulfilled for there to be a genuine plebiscite for the Native Hawaiian People:

1. A genuine plebiscite would have to be supervised by the United Nations Organization in order to guarantee a free, fair, impartial, and objective electoral process in accordance with historically recognized international standards and procedures;

2. Prior to the beginning of the plebiscite process, the United States government must withdraw its military forces, security agencies, and intelligence services (e.g., FBI, CIA, DEA, BATF, etc.) to their military bases and offices where they would be confined for the duration of the process, and their confinement must be monitored and ensured by the United Nations Organization;

3. After U.S. military forces and security agencies and intelligence services have been confined to their bases and offices, the Native Hawaiian People would need a substantial period of time in which they could engage freely and without fear of threat or intimidation in the processes of educating themselves and publicly debating among themselves as to the various options available, together with their meaningful access to the mainstream news media in Hawaii;

4. It must be guaranteed before the process begins that the will of the Native Hawaiian People is determinative and will be honored and respected whatever the results of such a plebiscite might be, including independence.

Based upon my reading of H.B.976, it does not appear that the process described therein would qualify as a genuine "plebiscite" in accordance with the generally recognized standards of international law and practice. Therefore, in order to ensure honesty, fairness and candor for the Native Hawaiian People, I would recommend that you seek to amend this legislation so as to call the process described therein something other than a "plebiscite."

Yours very truly,

Francis A. Boyle
Professor of International Law

•

April 5, 1996

Dear Native Hawaiian Friends:

I believe there has developed some confusion on the question of where I might stand on the proposed "native Hawaiian vote" that is currently being organized under the auspices of the Hawaiian Sovereignty Elections Council (HSEC). On March 5, 1995 I sent a formal Opinion Letter to the Honorable Pu'uhonua Kanahale for transmission to HSEC on the very narrow and precisely defined question: "...whether or not the elections to be supervised by the Hawaiian Sovereignty Elections Council as described in H.B. 976 would constitute a genuine 'plebiscite' in accordance with the generally recognized standards of international law and practice." I answered this question in the negative for the reasons indicated in the Letter. This Letter was never intended to endorse H.B. 976 or HSEC to any extent.

It has since come to my attention that on or about February 12, 1996, HSEC has deleted the word "plebiscite" and has substituted instead the words "native Hawaiian vote." Certainly the new language is preferable to the old language. But the substitution of the words "native Hawaiian vote" for "plebiscite" directly raises the question whether or not this "native Hawaiian vote" as currently organized by HSEC will either effectuate, or else abridge, the right of the Native Hawaiian People to self-determination under international law.

In Public Law Number 103-150 (the so-called Apology Resolution), Section 1(3) refers expressly to "...the rights of Native Hawaiians to self-determination..." In addition, a preambular clause in the Apology Resolution states quite clearly: "Whereas the indigenous Hawaiian people never directly relinquished their claims to their inherent sovereignty as a people or over their national lands to the United States, either through their monarchy or through a plebiscite or referendum..." It is obvious from this language that the United States Government, Congress, and President have now officially conceded that the Native Hawaiian People are entitled to "a plebiscite or referendum" in order to exercise "the rights of Native Hawaiians to self-determination." My March 9, 1995 Letter clearly states the four necessary preconditions for the Native Hawaiian People to exercise their right of self-determination under international law and practice. Quite obviously, H.B. 976 as originally drafted and also as currently amended to refer to a "native Hawaiian vote" does not fulfill any one of those four necessary preconditions.

Under these circumstances, you must understand that if you go forward with this "native Hawaiian vote" as currently organized by HSEC, there exists a very high probability that U.S. colonial occupation officials in Hawaii and Washington D.C., together with their supporters and sympathizers, will publicly proclaim that the HSEC "native Hawaiian vote" constituted a valid exercise of the right to self-determination by the Native Hawaiian People and therefore that the Native Hawaiian People have no further right to "a plebiscite or referendum" as required by international law and as recognized by the Apology Resolution. In other words, by going forward with HSEC's "native Hawaiian vote," the odds are quite high that you will be unjustly deprived of your right to "a plebiscite or referendum" and thus ultimately deprived of your "rights to self-determination" as required by international law and as recognized by the Apology Resolution.

Therefore, I must respectfully recommend in the strongest terms possible that you insist upon exercising your right to self-determination only by means of a "plebiscite" as defined by my March 9, 1995 Letter. The United States Government, Congress and President have already conceded that you are entitled to "a plebiscite or referendum" in order to exercise your "rights to self-determination." You must never agree to or go along with anything less than this. Otherwise, you risk losing your now internationally recognized "inherent sovereignty as a people."

May God always be with you.

Yours very truly,

Francis A. Boyle
Professor of International Law

NATION OF HAWAI'I
INDENPENDENT & SOVEREIGN NATION STATE

The Honorable John McCain
Chair, Indian Affairs Committee
United States Senate
Washington, DC
Fax No: 202-224-5429

Dear Senator:

Aloha. On behalf of my People, the Kanaka Hawai'i Maoli (Native Hawaiians), and in particular the Independent and Sovereign Nation State of Hawaii, I write to oppose in the strongest terms possible the Akaka legislation for the reasons indicated in the attached Lecture by our Counsel Professor Francis A. Boyle attached below.

I respectfully request that you:

1. Publicly oppose the Akaka legislation.
2. Speak out against it during the Senate debate.
3. Vote against it.

In addition, I also respectfully request that you enter my Letter and Professor Boyle's Lecture into the Congressional Record and circulate them to your colleagues.

In the event you have any questions, you may contact me directly or Professor Boyle at 217-333-7954. I look forward to hearing from you about this urgent request at your earliest convenience. Please confirm receipt of this message.

Respectfully Yours,

Pu'uhonua Bumpy D.K. Kanahele

Pu'uhonua Bumpy D.K. Kanahele

Head of State
Independent and Sovereign Nation State of Hawai'i

41-1300 Waikupanaha Street, Waimanalo, Hawai'i 96795 Tel: 808-259-9018 Fax: 808-259-9909 E-Mail: pu.uhonua@verizon.net

Prof. Francis A. Boyle Lecture
Regarding Akaka Legislation
Honolulu, 28 December 2004

A caveat to readers: This is an unofficial transcript provided for the information and convenience of our readers, and accuracy is not guaranteed. Areas that were inaudible to the transcriber are indicated with an ellipsis. For the most part these are small words or phrases that don't appear to change the meaning of the statements.

Pu'uhonua Bumpy D.K. Kanahele
Head of State
Independent and Sovereign Nation State of Hawaii

Aloha,

Thanks for coming ... between the holidays and da kine and all of that...

The Nation of Hawaii and the Office of Hawaiian Affairs are both co-sponsors in this event. We're actually doing a four-island in two-day talk ...

We just came in from Kaua'i, it was a good showing. But there's a lot of things that have sparked the independence movement in Hawaii. And, well, one, and the most important, the most important thing that happened to us, was 11 years ago, same day, December 28, almost the same time, that our guest speaker was here. There's a lot I'd like to say about him, he's actually been the only international lawyer I know who's been on the front lines across the world working with indigenous and native people all over the world.

So, once again I'd like to thank especially the Office of Hawaiian Affairs. You know for us there's been an independence movement for a long time, but we always got shut out. We felt that we were always getting shut out. It could be attitude both ways but we also felt too that the independence movement was always shortchanged financially where promotions would go one way and not the other way. So maybe this is a breakthrough... and the independence side can break through and actually start working with each other, working with the Office. You know the Office is also sponsoring the Hawaiian Coalition which is going on, they have talks and they're talking about sovereignty as well. But really this initiative is the beginning of an all-year initiative...Next year what we'd like to do is take the video, edit it down and go throughout the islands in 2005 and just get this message out.

We need balance on the playing field and we're not having that. This is why I'm glad that the Office actually... it was Clyde Namuo and several of the Trustees that actually said "Well, we got to do it, we're talking about the same thing and we have to get out and educate the people." And the Nation felt that it was more so important that we go back and look at the Apology Bill again because that is the foundation that even sparks and puts forward the Akaka Bill, not only independence. So right now it's education time. Let's hear it from somebody who eleven years ago was way ahead of his time ... And it's finally coming to a point where each one of us who is Hawaiian is going to have to make a choice. But me, as a Hawaiian, I don't want to be pushed into what I don't want or what I don't know. I like to hear from different views, different people, experts. which I've done over the years. I've heard a lot of different people speak.

There's only two sides, independence and being... that's it, there are no other alternatives. Some how some way you folks are going to have dig way inside your na'au and actually take the information and hopefully ... too and choose the side ....
So without further ado, I'd like to introduce you to our guest speaker, Professor Francis Anthony Boyle.

ALOHA!

I would like to express my thanks to my good friend Bumpy Kanahele and the Nation of Hawaii for inviting me, and also to the Office of Hawaiian Affairs for sponsoring my lectures here in Hawaii.

As you know in the 108th Congress, the Akaka legislation did not pass but it appears that it will be re-introduced into the new Congress probably along the lines of the Akaka-Abercrombie legislation we have now. And, just recently Senator Inouye has said he thinks it will pass in the 109th Congress. Well, with all due respect to Senator Inouye, I don't believe he is a prophet yet.

But, what I want to do here is to go through the Akaka-Abercrombie legislation as it died in the current session of Congress on the assumption it will be, as promised, introduced into the new session and give you my assessment of what it means for Kanaka Maoli. Understand it's your future that is at stake here, not mine. All I can do is come out and give you the benefit of my analysis and interpretation as I see the legislation. And then you will have to decide what to do.

What struck me right at the beginning of S344, that's the Senate version introduced by Senator Akaka and then the House version, HR665, by Congressman Abercrombie, there are slight differences, which I will comment on later. But what struck me right at the beginning was it says "...provide a process for recognition of the Native Hawaiian governing entity." And they used the word "entity," notice they did not use the word "government." They're not going to give Native Hawaiians a government and that's what they're going to give you is an entity. Well, I expect many of us here are trying to work for peace in the Middle East and one thing that is clear is that when Arab governments or states or people wish to express disrespect for Israel, instead of calling it the state of Israel or the government of Israel, they call it the Zionist entity.[1] It's a term of disrespect, not respect, to say we're going to give you an entity.

Certainly there is no way anyone can promote peace and reconciliation in the Middle East by referring to Israel as nothing more than the "Zionist entity" and I'm not exactly sure then how the United States Congress is going to promote peace and reconciliation with Kanaka Maoli by giving you a Kanaka entity. So that did strike me right off the top. Indeed it seems pretty clear this is very carefully drafted by lawyers who knew exactly what they were doing and how they were going to do it.

In the Findings clause, you'll note, they say in the Akaka draft, quote "Native Hawaiians, the native people of the Hawaiian archipelago that is now part of the United States." Well, isn't that the issue? The United States government says the Hawaiian Archipelago is part of the United States. But is it legally part of the United States, was it lawfully acquired by the United States? The Apology Resolution already said "No," and you have my detailed analysis of the Apology Resolution back on the table there. I'm not going to go back through the Apology Resolution at this point. But we're now at the next stage. Remember, the Apology Resolution called for reconciliation between Native Hawaiians and the United States ... And apparently now Akaka-

Abercrombie is their definition of what this reconciliation and settlement of claims, final settlement of claims, is all about.

This same Findings clause later continues with a baldfaced lie saying Native Hawaiians are indigenous native people of the United States. Well, of course that's preposterous. Native Hawaiians are the indigenous native people of Hawaii and the Kingdom of Hawaii, not the United States. The United States is 2600 miles in that direction according to my itinerary coming out here from Los Angeles last night.

International lawyers, and indeed the World Court and others, have what's known as the "Blue Water Rule." And the Blue Water Rule is quite simply when you have a metropolitan state separated by an ocean from another territory that they claim to be their own, the truth of the matter is that other territory is a colony, subject to the U.N. Decolonization Resolution. As you know, and indeed as my friend Kekuni Blaisdell has argued quite successfully so for many years, the United States illegally removed Hawaii from the Article 73 list of colonial territories that should have been decolonized and has refused to report and never applied the Decolonization Resolution to Hawaii, in violation of its obligation under the terms of the United Nations Charter —including Hawaii and many of the other colonial territories that it has now and still holds, separated by "blue water" from the continental United States.

Just because the United States says Hawaii is now part of the United States doesn't mean it's so as a matter of international law. At one point, France annexed Algeria and then determined by law that Algeria was a département of France, legally equivalent to Paris, which is also a département of France. And yet today, Algeria is an independent nation state and a member of the United Nations Organization. No one accepted the attempt by France to annex and "internalize" Algeria. And these same principles of international law surely apply to Hawaii.

Now, moving through the Abercrombie legislation, it talks about treaties between the United States and the Kingdom of Hawaii, most of which were violated by the United States of America. Here, mostly importantly, the Treaty of Friendship, Commerce and Navigation of 1849 that guaranteed, the United States guaranteed, the Kingdom of Hawaii "perpetual peace and amity." And that treaty was never terminated by either party. So technically as a matter of law, it still exists. Today, the United States is still supposed to be promising the Kingdom of Hawaii and Kanaka Maoli perpetual peace and amity. And I should point out, that treaty, and all the other treaties that are violated, are the supreme law of the land under Article 6 of the United States Constitution. So they violated their own Constitution as well.

Now, there was an interesting result when Keanu Sai and I sued the United States in the United States Supreme Court under the original jurisdiction clause in 1998 on the 100th anniversary of the illegal annexation of Hawaii by the United States. Keanu and I pleaded all of these treaties, every one of them, and we demanded that the United States Supreme Court order the United States federal government to restore the Kingdom of Hawaii and, in addition, to pay reparations for all the harm that has been inflicted on the Kingdom of Hawaii including the violation of numerous treaties.

What happened in this lawsuit surprised even me. The Justices of the United States Supreme Court met three times and eventually they rejected the entire lawsuit, refused to let us even file the lawsuit, and returned our filing fee, which is almost without precedent. They always want money to pay those bills. Why did they return our filing fee and all of our documents? I had about a 45-minute conversation, argument, call it what you want, with the Deputy Clerk of the Court in which he said well, they had him call up the State Department and the State Department said that the United States does not recognize the Kingdom of Hawaii and therefore the Supreme Court has decided not to let us even docket our papers and accept our fee. The reason is that there is a black-letter rule of U.S. Constitutional law that non-recognized sovereigns cannot have access to United States courts.

Now what I found curious about that is that apparently they were taking the position, the Supreme Court Justices, that the Kingdom of Hawaii was a non-recognized sovereign state. In other words, we were a sovereign state but we just weren't recognized by the State Department. That's a very interesting result in that proceeding. And I do want to commend Keanu Sai for doing so much hard work to get this very important and precedential proceeding and ruling by the United States

Supreme Court to commemorate the 100th anniversary of the illegal annexation of Hawaii.

Now, the Akaka legislation then continues by conceding yes, by means of these treaties, the United States recognized the independence of the Kingdom of Hawaii. That's correct. And as I pointed out they also guaranteed perpetual peace and amity—that means forever. They afforded full diplomatic recognition to the Kingdom of Hawaii and as I said that treaty of peace and amity was never terminated by either party, it was never formally terminated. It is still the supreme law of the land in the United States under the United States Constitution. And this is what Keanu and I tried to argue in the United States Supreme Court, if they had docketed our papers, we would have been there arguing this point. But it raises the issue then that the Kingdom of Hawaii itself, as a state, was never properly terminated. In other words, it still exists legally. There are still treaties, the Kingdom of Hawaii is still a party to these treaties, not only with the United States but also with a fairly large number of other states.

You recall your Kings and your Queen were very foresighted in establishing diplomatic relations and treaty relations with a large number of other states at the time. Now, the haoles said "Oh, this is an unnecessary expenditure of funds," but your Kings and your Queen understood that this would be a way to further solidify the existence of the Kingdom of Hawaii as a state under international law and practice. And we have to keep that clear. Later on, I'll make a distinction between a state and a government. In international law, that's a critical distinction, a state and a government. So today I think we have our state, it's the Kingdom of Hawaii. We don't have a government but we do have a state and we have treaties.

Akaka then moves on by going back to the Apology Resolution concessions. It says yes again, the Kanaka Maoli never relinquished their claims to inherent sovereignty, that's a right as a people over their lands, either by the monarchy itself, we know that they never did, or plebiscite or referendum. You never validly surrendered any of your rights to the United States of America and notice they use the word sovereignty, you have the sovereignty. They conceded that in the Apology Resolution. The sovereignty is that of the Kanaka Maoli not the

United States. Indeed the United States from the perspective of international law as of circa 1893 up until 1898 for sure, was and still is nothing more than a belligerent occupant of Hawaii. It invaded, it conquered and it intended to annex but at all times it remained a belligerent occupant subject to the laws of war and the laws of belligerent occupation. And what does that mean? Occupation even annexation, cannot change sovereignty. The sovereignty resides in the hands of the displaced sovereign, which in this case is the Kingdom of Hawaii and the Kanaka Maoli people. The United States simply cannot go out and annex Hawaii and hold it unto themselves. That sovereignty is still in the hands of the Kanaka Maoli and it still resides within the Kingdom of Hawaii and basically they do concede that in the Apology Resolution and the Akaka draft bill.

Now, they then move on in these Findings clauses and point out that Native Hawaiians give expression to their rights as native people to self-determination, self-government and economic self-sufficiency. Notice here they see self-determination as it is seen under international law and practice. The Kanaka Maoli have a right of self-determination. What does that mean? The Kanaka Maoli determine for yourselves what is your future. Do you want to restore that Kingdom of Hawaii? Do you want to become a state of the United States of America? Do you want something like Puerto Rico has in its relations with the United States as a Commonwealth? But the question of self-determination is for you to decide, not them. And the Kanaka Maoli, as even the Apology Resolution and the Akaka legislation concede, have never had the opportunity to validly exercise your right of self-determination in accordance with international law and practice. And they're conceding that right of self-determination here.

Now, you might say "Well, why are they giving us all these concessions? Aren't they doing us a favor?" And my reading of the legislation is No! The reason they're making these concessions is so that at the end of the day, assuming Akaka passes into law, they can then say "Well, now the Akaka legislation, this is their exercise of self-determination and they're going along with this procedure for the Native Hawaiian entity and they are now going to exercise their right of self-determination and their inherent sovereignty within the context of our entity that we are giving them that we will not even bother to call a government. We're not even going to give the Native Hawaiians a government, we're just going to give them an entity and that's their sovereignty, that's their self-determination and then we'll stop at that. That can be their choice."

Now they also point out of course the Native Hawaiians already provide healthcare, education, employment, children services, language etc, etc. This is the way you build a state or rebuild a state or restore a state: from the ground up, not the top down. No one's going to give you a state, especially not the United States of America. You have to build that state from the ground up by providing basic services to your own people.

Look at the way the Palestinians have done this in occupied Palestine. They do not rely on the Israeli occupational authorities to provide any services to their people because they know they're not going to get it. So the Palestinians have to go out and find a way to build education, healthcare, nutrition, training etc., to their own people living under a very brutal military occupation regime but they're building it. They're building their state from the ground up, not the top down. And you Kanaka Maoli have all the elements and the rudiments to do this, you are in the process of doing this. You just have to do more and do it better and be more organized and more effective.

Later on, the Akaka legislation then says, quote, "this act provides a process within the framework of Federal Law for Native Hawaiian people to exercise their inherent rights." Well again, that is the agenda here. They want to divert and limit all of your rights of self-determination, sovereignty, your right to the restoration of the Kingdom of Hawaii, all within this process that will lead to nothing more than a Kanaka entity, all determined by United States Federal Law. You'll note there's no reference at all here to international law except to the treaties which they've already conceded they have violated.

But, rather than specify what are your rights under international law, they try to limit them to federal law, United States Federal Law. Now, of course from the perspective of international law, not United States Federal Law, if you have a violation of these treaties, and Keanu Sai and I tried to argue this at the U.S. Supreme Court and in the papers we filed it's quite sensibly argued, and as I pointed out, the appropriate remedy for treaty violations is restitution even as recognized by the World Court. And I pointed this out in my analysis of the Apology Resolution. And by the Latin terminology *restitutio in integrum*—return the situation to the way it existed before the treaty violation.

In other words the United States has an obligation to restore the Kingdom of Hawaii, to return the situation to what it was when it signed that 1849 Treaty of Friendship, Commerce and Navigation and promised the Kingdom of Hawaii perpetual peace and amity.

That is the real remedy ... under international law and practice, not setting up some bogus little entity which, as then we'll see, has very little rights to begin with and powers. Yet they will then claim that this is your final exercise of self-determination and sovereignty within our little straightjacket—the "final solution" for the Kanaka Maoli. That's what they have in mind here.

Now, they say they will give you a council, Native Hawaiian interim governing council. Here you can see again they borrowed this language, this idea from the Middle East peace process. This is what the Israelis promised the Palestinians in the Oslo Accords. I was their Lawyer at the time and it was a provisional interim governing council that they promised them. But notice it's not a government, the adjective is very cleverly drafted. They tried to do this same stuff to the Palestinians too and instead of saying it's a government they put it "governing," but it modifies "council" so it's nothing more than a council. Well, you know, the Boy Scouts have their council too, the Boy Scouts Council. Hey, I'm a former Eagle Scout, I have nothing against the Boy Scouts but you know we're talking here of the future of Kanaka Maoli. So they knew what they were doing. They could have easily reversed this and said yeah we're going to give you a councilior government but instead they're giving you a governing council. So Governing was put in there to sort of make you think well, you're really getting a government with governmental powers but you're not getting any of this. You'll get a council, like the Boy Scouts.

And finally, it turns out that this council that they're going to give Kanaka Maoli will be subject to the jurisdiction and control of the Secretary of the Interior, not the Secretary of State but the

Secretary of the Interior, again the assumption being that Hawaii is somehow interior to the United States. Well, you know, all you have to do is look at a globe and you'll find out that Hawaii is not interior to the United States. But, put that issue aside. Who is the Secretary of the Interior today? The Honorable Gale Norton.

The Honorable Gale Norton is a member of the right-wing racist reactionary Federalist Society.[2] And it was the Federalist Society lawyers that organized *Rice v. Cayetano*.[3] They were the ones behind *Rice v Cayetano*. They sponsored the litigation, they argued the litigation, they took it all the way to the United States Supreme Court. Four of those Justices were members of the Federalist Society and Justice Rehnquist ... a fellow traveler. They gave you *Rice v Cayetano*, argued that O.H.A. was racist, and therefore the haoles get to vote for the O.H.A. trustees.

So under this legislation, they are going to turn Kanaka Maoli over to the tender mercies of Federalist Society lawyers in the Department of the Interior, Norton being one, and most of her legal staff that she brought in with her are all Federalist Society lawyers. These are the people that brought you *Rice v Cayetano* and this assault on O.H.A. Do you really think that the Secretary of the Interior will care one wit about the Kanaka Maoli?

We know for a fact that the Department of the Interior has looted and plundered hundreds of millions of dollars of the so-called trust fund that the United States set up for American Indians. We don't know the exact figure because a federal district judge, despite repeated orders to get an accounting, has been told by Secretary Norton, "Take a hike." And it does not look likely at all that we're ever going to get a figure on how much money was looted and plundered by the Department of the Interior and the Secretary of the Interior from American Indians. Well, what do you think they're going to do to Kanaka Maoli when they get their tentacles around you, if they've already done this to American Indians? Well, they're not going to treat you any better, I think, than American Indians. You'll probably get similar treatment, looting and plundering.

Moving on then, it's very interesting, they then refer to 150 federal laws recognizing that Native Hawaiians have an inherent right to autonomy in their internal affairs. Well, already that conclusion is undercut in recognizing the right of self-determination, which they have conceded in the Apology

Resolution. Sure, if all you want is autonomy in your internal affairs, fine, that is for you to decide but self-determination, which they have conceded legally for the Kanaka Maoli, means a lot more than that. It means that if you want the Kingdom of Hawaii to be restored as a state, to have your independence, that is your right pursuant to self-determination.

But here they are significantly trying to cut it down. Not only are they trying to cut it down from self-determination to autonomy, but they have further limited autonomy. Again, I've seen the State Department try to do the same thing with the Palestinians, they further limited autonomy by saying an autonomy only in their internal affairs, no other autonomy. Well, at least the Palestinians were given autonomy. There was no attempt made to say we'll only give you autonomy in your internal affairs. So notice they cut down self-determination first to autonomy, and then they limited the autonomy to only your internal affairs. So, basically you're getting less than even the Israelis were prepared to give the Palestinians which, again, in my opinion, does not augur well for the future.

It's very interesting that finally we get to the governing matter in Section 7, it says "The right of the Native Hawaiian people to organize for their common welfare and [to] adopt appropriate organic documents is recognized by the United States." So, the United States is recognizing the right of the Hawaiian people to adopt "documents." Notice it doesn't say "laws," they're not giving you the right to adopt laws. It doesn't even say regulations which are somewhat less than laws. All you get is the right to adopt documents. Now that's nice but the State Department and the Israelis were even prepared to give the Palestinians in the Oslo Accords more.

Now what is a "document"? Well, the law has a definition of a "document." I have a piece of Kleenex here and now I'm going to date it and put "IOU 5¢" on there and I'll sign my name.[4] And all of sudden ... that piece of Kleenex becomes a document as far as the law is concerned. But you know and I know it's still a piece of Kleenex. That's all they're giving you here. You can adopt whatever documents you want, you can bring in all the signed Kleenex you want, but that's all you get, as far as we're concerned. Now you could bring in the phone book here for Honolulu, that's great, but we will not recognize your right to do anything more than that. You can't make laws. You can't make regulations. So in other words, you don't have legal authority really to do anything but you can have as many pieces of Kleenex as you want.

Whoever drafted this was very careful, very clever, I'm sure it was probably those same Federalist Society lawyers over there in the Department of the Interior who gave you *Rice v Cayetano*. It wouldn't surprise me at all.

Well, then we get into the election of this council and it turns out of course that the whole determination of who gets to elect the council is under the control of the Secretary of the Interior. Well I've already commented on our current Secretary of the Interior, but, you know, let's suppose that we get St. Peter as the Secretary of the Interior. Well, it's not the right of St. Peter to decide for the Kanaka Maoli who is Kanaka Maoli. Under the right of self-determination of people, it is for the Kanaka Maoli to decide who are Kanaka Maoli, not the Secretary of the Interior, let alone St. Peter or anyone else.

That's the essence of self-determination, you decide who you are. The United States Federal government has no right to determine who are Kanaka Maoli. Now I know they try to do that all the time but in the end doesn't mean it's lawful, that doesn't mean it's right under international law. Self-determination means you decide, they don't decide.

Now we get to the powers of this council. And, here, two things, first the council only represents individual Kanaka Maolis, that's it. It doesn't represent anyone or anything else, especially and including land. It has no control over land. None. Indeed, if there was any doubt about that, Section 2 says "council shall have no powers other than the powers given to the council under this act." Well again that contradicts the principle of self-determination and inherent sovereignty. The Kanaka Maoli should be able to decide what powers this council has, not the United States Congress. And yet they've made it very clear, all you get is what limited powers we give you. And what is that? Well, the council can represent individual Kanaka Maolis, and it's very interesting the way it's drafted, it doesn't say the council may represent the Kanaka Maoli people, no, the council will only represent individuals on this list drawn up by the Secretary of the Interior. So it will represent individuals but not the people, not the Kanaka Maoli themselves, as the government of the Kingdom of Hawaii. So what they're trying to do to you here is atomize you. To eliminate your status as a people, under international law and practice, with the right of self-determination.

And they do this all the time. Up in Geneva at the Indigenous Peoples Forum they've refused to recognize that indigenous peoples are peoples, they call them indigenous persons. Why? Well, because a people have a right of self-determination and the United States doesn't want indigenous peoples to have a right of self-determination, so they just call them indigenous persons. .....an atomized group not the people ....

Moreover, as I've said, it's clear that this council has no control over land. None, it isn't there. Later on they say, well, at some point in the indefinite future we might consider giving this council some control over some land, but we're not making any promises. That's it. Well, again, very similar to what happened to the Palestinians in the Camp David Accords, where the Camp David Accords called for autonomy for the Palestinian people, again, what they're giving you is less than that here. After Camp David was over, the Prime Minister of Israel, Menachem Begin, said that's only autonomy for the people and not for the land.

It only calls for autonomy for the people. So you get a council that represents persons but no control over the land. Now later on President Carter contradicted that and said no, it calls for autonomy for the people and the land because otherwise what good is autonomy? If you can't control people and land, what good is it? Unfortunately in the Oslo Accords, again, I served as lawyer ..., that's exactly what the Palestinians got. They got a council, an autonomy, a people and no control over the land. And that's what they're trying to give you here. It will be a council that represents individuals, not even Kanaka Maoli as a whole, and with no power over land.

And indeed at this point, if you sever the people from the land, we'll have the people over here and the land over there and maybe at some point in the indefinite future, we might join them, maybe we won't. It might be a smaller amount, it might be a larger amount—who knows? We'll decide that when it's time to get to that issue.

And indeed that's made very clear in the section about negotiations that at some point in the future there will be a talk about transfer of lands ... So, this council has no land, no natural resources, no assets, it can't tax. So what effective power does it have, except to represent this atomized group of individual Kanaka Maolis?

And finally, to add insult to injury, having started out treating you in the same reprehensible way they treat American Indians, Senator Akaka says to the Indian Affairs Council in the Senate, "But by the way, you Kanaka Maoli, even though we're going to treat you like Indians we're not going to give you any of the benefits ..." That's made very clear in Section 9b, "Nothing contained in this act provides authorization for eligibility to anything run by the Bureau of Indian Affairs," which is also determined and under the jurisdiction and control of the Secretary of the Interior.

Now before I move on to an alternative, I do want to say just a few words about the Abercrombie draft bill in the House. When it comes to enacting U.S. legislation, there's usually a bill in the Senate, there's a bill in the House, there are differences between them. Assuming they both pass, they go to a conference and get reconciled .....

In many areas Abercrombie just tracks Akaka but there are some significant differences that I think need to be commented on because at the end of the day, if this legislation passes, you could be ending up with the Abercrombie version instead of Akaka's, or some hybrid combination.

..... Congressman Abercrombie referred his Bill to the Committee on Resources. Well, at least Senator Akaka referred his bill to the Committee on Indian Affairs, and he's treating the Kanaka Maoli like human beings but similarly to American Indians. With the Abercrombie Bill, you'll be in there with the streams and the rivers and the coal mines, and things of that nature. And so obviously they're thinking of you as a natural resource. You're valuable to the tourists so they have to think of you Kanaka Maoli as an economic resource here to attract tourists so that we haole can make money. So that's all made very clear right in the beginning of the Abercrombie legislation.

And of course he does again track all the treaties that they have violated going through Akaka and the Apology Resolution but what I really wanted to comment on here was the one section in Abercrombie that is not in Akaka, that in my opinion really gives the whole game away. And that's Section 3 on Ceded Lands "Those lands which were ceded to the United States by the Republic of Hawaii and which were later transferred to the State of Hawaii."

Well, one second, they're conceding in this very Bill that all United States lands that they got here in Hawaii came from the Republic of Hawaii but they've already admitted that the Republic of Hawaii illegally overthrew the Kingdom of Hawaii. They've admitted and conceded this. So in other words, the Republic of Hawaii never had valid title over any lands here in Hawaii to begin with. That's clear. It was a thief, the Republic of Hawaii, and this was thievery by which they stole your lands. And they're conceding that, yes, that the United States took the lands stolen from the Kanaka Maoli by the Republic of Hawaii and called them their own and then transferred some of them to the State of Hawaii. But that still doesn't alter the fundamental fact of theft. The United States has no valid title to any of these lands to begin with because they're conceding they got what they got from the Republic of Hawaii and that is clearly illegal theft.

So, this legislation we've got here, if it is passed, will try to quiet title to all of that land. They know there is a problem out here with all title in Hawaii because it all goes back to this original act of theft in 1893. How do you establish valid title under those circumstances when they've conceded it's based on an act of thievery to begin with? And this legislation will try to quiet that title so that people can then say "Well yes, now we can convey valid title."

Keanu Sai did a lot of work on this issue .... the very valid legal issue, well how do you get title out here in Hawaii when so much of it goes back to this act of thievery in 1893?

You Kanaka Maoli will have to decide where you stand on Akaka/Abercrombie. I've given you my analysis about it but from an international law perspective. Certainly I think some points are clear: one, the existence of the Kingdom of Hawaii as a state under international law and practice was never validly extinguished, it's still there, in essence. It needs to be revived and restored. Indeed, as I pointed out in that Treaty of Friendship, Commerce and Navigation, the United States promised perpetual peace and amity and the correct remedy is

restitutio in integrum—return the situation to what it was before the violation in 1893, which the United States conceded in the Apology Resolution was conducted by their agents. In other words, they're responsible for what happened in 1893.
This is why Bumpy Kanahele and the Ohana Council and others issued their Proclamation of the Restoration of the Independence of the Sovereign Nation State of Hawaii on January 16th, 1994. Notice it was not a declaration of independence, you already had your independence. Independence did not need to be declared—what needed to be done was to restore that which had been stolen.

Now there are 4 requirements for a state under international law and practice: (1) a permanent population; (2) territory; (3) a functioning government; and (4) the capacity to conduct international relations.

Well, in this case, we already have a state, the Kingdom of Hawaii, that was never validly terminated—it still exists there in most degrees.

Second, a permanent population. We have that, the Kanaka Maoli. Despite all the efforts to diminish your numbers, including outright acts of genocide, you're still here and you're still on your land. The essence of sovereignty is a people still living on their land and still asserting their rights and that gives you enormous power in dealing with the haoles. They know who you are, this is your land and your people are on it.

Third, a government. And here we come to the problem that I think confronts Kanaka Maoli today, at least in my opinion, you probably have a different assessment, but I am approaching this as an international lawyer. We have a state but we don't have a government. We have a state—it's the Kingdom of Hawaii but there is no functioning government for the Kingdom of Hawaii that represents all Kanaka Maoli.

We have, as you know, several different organizations that have drafted constitutions that represent certain segments of the Kanaka Maoli. But in my opinion what we really need now is a government of national unity for the Kingdom of Hawaii. We need all the disparate groups and factions to come together.

Again, this was the situation that confronted the Palestinians 35 years ago. There were many different groups, and organizations, and factions. And yet eventually the late

President Arafat and his organization Fatah were able to pull them all together, and by the process of consensus and debate and argument, they set up a government. Today the Palestinian state is recognized by about 130 states, starting out with nothing in 1964. And they have de facto, but not yet de jure, U.N. membership. [5] The only reason they are not yet a U.N. member is the threat of a veto by the United States government. But even then, President Bush himself has stated that his ultimate objective is a Palestinian state.

Now of course it's not for President Bush to give the Palestinians a state, they have their own state, they're making their own state. Palestinians struggle for their own state just as Kanaka Maoli will have to struggle for their own state. Even General Sharon, the Prime Minister of Israel, has admitted in public debate in their parliament, the Knesset, that the Palestinians already have their own state.

So they made a lot of progress but they had to put together a government that united them all, an effective government that could represent the interests of all the people and move forward from there. This was done in a democratic way despite the rigors of military occupation that is still inflicted upon them today.

So we need, I think from my perspective, but you have to decide this, a government of national unity for the Kingdom of Hawaii that pulls together all the different groups and organizations and movements, etc. with a common platform and program and speaks for as many Kanaka Maoli as possible. And then, build that state from the ground up. You're not going to get your state by going to court. Keanu Sai and I tried going to the U.S. Supreme Court. I felt, even though I thought the odds were quite high, I thought the effort had to be made, especially to commemorate the 100th anniversary of the illegal annexation, we had to do something and Keanu and I did. Build that state from the ground up with this government of national unity.

And then, the fourth requirement for recognition as a state: the capacity to conduct international relations. To go out with this government of national unity and take off where the Kingdom left off, that is, to try to re-establish diplomatic and treaty relations with all those states and those governments that the Kingdom had diplomatic relations with as of 1893. And again, your Kings and your Queen knew full well the critical importance of doing so. So you have to go back and pick up where the Kingdom left off in 1893. Re-establish those relations, re-assert those treaties and then try to extend it. And do both processes at the same time, the provisional government building the state, helping to build that state from the ground up, and then second, seeking that international recognition and relations as best as possible.

Obviously this is a long-term agenda, the problem has been here since at least 1893, if not going back to circa the Bayonet Consitution.[6] It's not going to resolve tomorrow. But look at the tremendous progress the Palestinians have made in just 35 years. I see the tremendous progress Kanaka Maoli have made just in these last 11 years. I've been here since then but the last time we talked about human rights and now it's the question of independence and sovereignty. So there has been a lot of progress. But in my opinion there has to be a lot more. The next step I would recommend you to consider is to move forward on this government of national unity.

Answers to Questions

1. The United States government has incriminated itself under international law for the crimes it has committed against Kanaka Maoli and the Hawaiian Kingdom. The appropriate remedy here, under International Law, is restitution in full, that is, restoration of the Hawaiian Kingdom and also payment of damages.
2. Rather than surrender your rights under international law, as Akaka/Abercrombie is calling for you to do, you should insist on all of your rights under International Law.
3. Gandhi, by means of his *Satyagraha*, "truth force", was able to throw the mighty British Empire out of the entire Indian subcontinent without violence.
4. I think there's grounds to believe that the Kanaka Maoli, pursuing the Spirit of Aloha and *Satyagraha*, could do the same to the United States Empire.
5. You have to stand up to them, in a peaceful, non-violent way, as Kanaka Maoli living on your own land, and insist on your rights. And they will have to recognize that, just as ultimately the British with all their power, had to recognize Gandhi and his demand that they go home. America is obligated to go home and evacuate and leave Hawaii.

6. You, the Kanaka Maoli, and your Kupuna, have to decide what to do, not me. At best, lawyers can give advice, counsel, occasionally representation, but that's it. That is not going to solve your problem.
7. Kanaka Maoli must derive the strength and the power and the authority to make clear the rights they have in dealing with this intimidation, and indeed outright genocide, that the United States has indeed inflicted on Kanaka Maoli.
8. If you read the Genocide Convention, it clearly says one of the acts of genocide is deliberately inflicting on a people conditions of life calculated to bring about their physical destruction in whole or in part. And clearly that's the history of what the United States government has tried to do to the Kanaka Maoli. And in my opinion, Akaka/Abercrombie will only accelerate that process. So you have to stand up for your rights and tell the United States "these are our rights, we demand them, this is our land, go home, you have inflicted genocide upon us, and we've had enough of it, and we've had enough of you."

I wrote on the following Kleenex during one of my anti-Akaka-Bill Lectures.

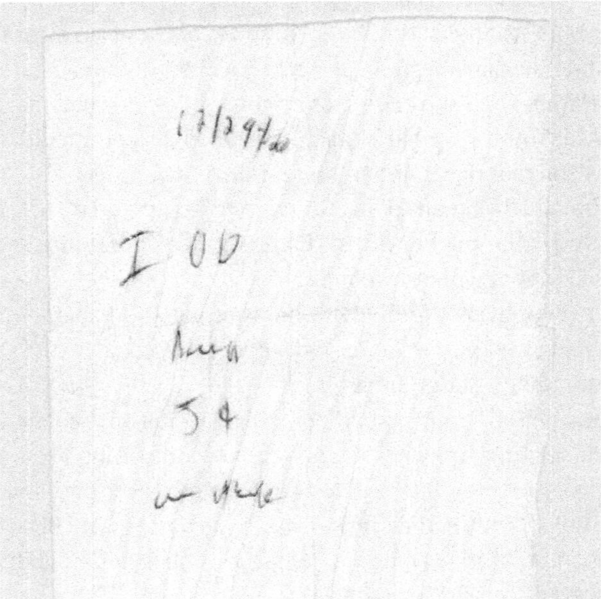

ENDNOTES

1 *See* Francis A. Boyle, Palestine, Palestinians and International Law (2003) *and* Breaking All the Rules (2008) *and* The Palestinian Right of Return under International Law (2011).

2 *See* George E. Curry & Trevor W. Coleman, *Special Report: Hijacking Justice,* Emerge, October 1999.

3 Rice v. Cayetano, 528 U.S. 495, 120 S. Ct. 1044 (2000). Haoles can vote to elect the Board of Trustees of the Office of Hawaiian Affairs (O.H.A.).

4 *See infra* at the end of this chapter for a picture of this original piece of Kleenex/document that I used to illustrate this point during my Lecture that I saved.

5 On November 29, 2012 the United Nations General Assembly determined that Palestine was officially a United Nations Observer State. *See* Dennis Bernstein, *An Interview with Professor Francis Boyle,* Counterpunch.org, Dec. 4, 2012.

6 *See* David Keanu Sai, Ph.D., UA MAU KE EA, Sovereignty Endures: An Overview of the Political and Legal History of the Hawaiian Islands 59-69 (2011).

CHAPTER 6

RESTORING THE KINGDOM OF HAWAII

Kanakamaolilandustan Redux

As of 2010 both the American Akaka and Abercrombie U.S. federal legislation to enable Kanakamaolilandustan still remained dead in the poisonous waters of the American Congress. Then American Representative Neil Abercrombie decided to leave the American House of Representatives in order to run successfully for the colonial administrative governorship of the illegal American state of Hawaii. So not surprisingly, soon after his installation as the colonial administrative "governor" of the illegal American state of Hawaii in December of 2010, Mr. Abercrombie signed into Hawaiian state law the American Hawaiian Colonial Law Act 195 on July 6, 2011.

Mr. Abercrombie's newest version of creating Kanakamaolilandustan by the illegal American state of Hawaii was basically a reworking of his federal Native Hawaiian Government Reorganization Act, H. R. 2314, 111th Congress (2010), whose predecessor was already extensively critiqued in the preceding chapter of this book. The illegal American state of Hawaii Colonial Act 195 (2011) called for the establishment of a "Native Hawaiian roll commission" whose purpose would be to prepare and maintain a "roll" of whomever they deemed to be "qualified Native Hawaiians." This illegal American state of Hawaii "roll" of "qualified Native Hawaiians" certified by their good-housekeeping seal-of-approval would then be able "to participate in the organization of the Native Hawaiian governing entity." This process would be commenced by "the organization of a convention of qualified Native Hawaiians, established for the purpose of organizing themselves." The prorogued American state-initiated process then became an involuntary "enrollment" process. The Convention is currently scheduled to be taking place in early 2015.

I will not repeat here any of my fatal criticisms of this latest reiteration of Kanakamaolilandustan that is now being articulated by the illegal American state of Hawaii and its colonial administrative governor Mr. Abercrombie in American Hawaiian Colonial Act 195 (2011) that have already been set forth at great length in the preceding chapter of this book. Creating Kanakamaolilandustan by the American state of Hawaii to get around the now-deadlocked and poisoned American Congress was obviously and transparently the intention of the drafters of American Hawaiian Colonial Act 195 (2011) from the get-go. For that very reason, many Kanaka Maoli leaders, Ohana, Sovereignty groups, organizations, and individuals refused to participate in the enrollment process but were nevertheless "enrolled" against their wishes.

International Legal Jiu-jitsu Against Kanakamaolilandustan

I would like to respectfully recommend that for those Kanaka Maoli who have as a matter of good faith and conscience decided to enroll for and/or to participate in the forthcoming Convention "for the purpose of organizing themselves" in order to establish "the Native Hawaiian governing entity," that at that forthcoming Convention they vote to restore the Kingdom of Hawaii. In other words, that the Kanaka Maoli at the forthcoming Convention "organize themselves" by voting to restore the Kingdom of Hawaii. Those Kanaka Maoli who choose to attend the forthcoming Convention should organize themselves therein in such a way as to determine that "the Native Hawaiian governing entity" contemplated by American Hawaiian Colonial Act 195 (2011) shall be the restored Kingdom of Hawaii. That result would be consistent with the operative language of American Hawaiian Colonial Act 195 (2011) even though Kanakamaolilandustan was the original intended result of the drafters of American Hawaii Colonial Act 195 (2011)—and certainly not the Restoration of the Kingdom of Hawaii.

I respectfully submit that those Kanaka Maoli who attend the forthcoming Convention must turn the entire process of and momentum behind American Hawaiian Colonial Act 195 (2011) against the illegal American colonial state of Hawaii and against the illegal belligerent occupying power of Hawaii that is the United States of America. The

Kanaka Maoli must perform political jiu-jitsu against their American occupiers and other haole oppressors by means of international law. Furthermore, those Kanaka Maoli who have already been involuntarily enrolled on the American Hawaiian Colonial Act 195 (2011) "roll" of "qualified Native Hawaiians" might want to consider attending the forthcoming Convention for the sole purpose of voting to restore the Kingdom of Hawaii.

Section 2 of American Hawaiian Colonial Act 195 (2011) provides that the "Purpose" of the legislation is as follows:

> § -2 **Purpose**. The purpose of this chapter is to provide for and to implement the recognition of the Native Hawaiian people by means and methods that will facilitate their self-governance, including the establishment of, or the amendment to, programs, entities, and other matters pursuant to law that relate, or affect ownership, possession, or use of lands by the Native Hawaiian people, and by further promoting their culture, heritage, entitlements, health, education, and welfare.

I respectfully submit for the consideration of the Kanaka Maoli that the one and only one way that all these objectives can be obtained is for them to vote at the forthcoming Convention for the Restoration of the Kingdom of Hawaii.

Moreover, American Hawaiian Colonial Act 195 (2011) further states: "It is also the State's desire to support the continuing development of a reorganized Native Hawaiian governing entity and, ultimately, the federal recognition of Native Hawaiians." **That is just fine!** At the forthcoming Convention the Kanaka Maoli must vote to restore the Kingdom of Hawaii. Then at the forthcoming Convention the Kanaka Maoli must demand that the illegal American State of Hawaii support the restored Kingdom of Hawaii as the "reorganized Native Hawaiian governing entity." In addition, at the forthcoming Convention the Kanaka Maoli must also demand that the illegal American State of Hawaii "support...the federal recognition of Native Hawaiians" by backing them up in their efforts to obtain formal bilateral diplomatic recognition as a de jure State for the restored Kingdom of Hawaii by the United States Federal Government. Next, at the forthcoming Convention the Kanaka Maoli must demand that the illegal American state of Hawaii back them up in their efforts to have the United States Federal Government revive and resume all those treaties that the United States of America had concluded with the Kingdom of Hawaii as of 1893. Finally, at the forthcoming Convention the Kanaka Maoli must demand that the illegal American state of Hawaii back them up in their efforts to expel the United States Federal Government from the Kingdom of Hawaii. **Yankee go home! Free Hawaii!**

The Restoration of the Kingdom of Hawaii

In this manner the restored Kingdom of Hawaii will constitute the legal continuation of the 1893 Kingdom of Hawaii whose existence as a State was never lawfully terminated and which therefore continues to exist as a State today under public international law for all the reasons set forth in the previous chapters of this book. It is a basic maxim of all domestic legal systems around the world today and therefore of public international law according to Article 38(1)(c) of the Statute of the International Court of Justice: *Ex iniuria ius non oritur!* Right does not arise from injury!

In this regard, during my December 2004 lecture tour around Hawaii against the American Akaka/Abercrombie U.S. federal legislation, as my suggested alternative to their obscene and perverse vision of Kanakamaolilandustan, I briefly discussed the reasons behind and the requirements for the Restoration of the Kingdom of Hawaii under international law and practice. Let me recapitulate those arguments here and expand upon them. There are four requirements for the restored Kingdom of Hawaii under international law and practice: (1) permanent population; (2) territory; (3) a functioning government; and (4) the capacity to conduct international relations.

Prelude: Kanaka Maoli Already Ahead of the Game for Nation-Statehood

To begin with, as a preliminary point, and as well-established matters of both fact and of law, in the case of Hawaii the Kanaka Maoli already have the Kingdom of Hawaii that was never validly terminated in 1893. This 1893 Kingdom of Hawaii still exists today as a subject of public international law. This 1893 Kingdom of Hawaii only needs to be effectively restored on a functioning basis—both internationally and domestically. This existential act of Restoration of the 1893 Kingdom of Hawaii can and must be done by those Kanaka Maoli attending the forthcoming Convention.

The United States of America is nothing more than the illegal belligerent occupant of the 1893 Kingdom of Hawaii subject to the international laws of war including therein the international laws of belligerent occupation. Sovereignty has always resided in and still resides in the hands of the Kanaka Maoli themselves—and certainly not in the United States of America to any extent. The Kanaka Maoli have the right to restore their 1893 Kingdom of Hawaii, and then to demand that the illegal belligerent occupying forces of the United States—civilian, military, and paramilitary (e.g., F.B.I., C.I.A., N.S.A., B.A.T.F., D.H.S., I.C.E., T.S.A., D.O.A., I.R.S., etc.) evacuate Hawaii immediately—lock, stock, and barrel. I respectfully recommend to those Kanaka Maoli who attend the forthcoming Convention that they do just that, then and there. **Yankee go home! Free Hawaii!**

1. Population

The first requirement for the restored Kingdom of Hawaii under international law and practice is that of a permanent population. The Kanaka Maoli have already fulfilled that requirement. All of today's Kanaka Maoli are the direct and lineal descendants of the original Polynesian settlers and inhabitants of Hawaii and thus automatically can and should become citizens of the restored Kingdom of Hawaii. By contrast, the American-imposed categories of "blood-quantum" are racist and genocidal and therefore are entitled to absolutely no recognition or respect whatsoever under public international law and international human rights law.

Despite all the American efforts to reduce the numbers of the Kanaka Maoli—including outright acts of genocide as well as the ongoing slow-motion genocide that continues as of today—the Kanaka Maoli are still living on their ancestral land of Hawaii. The essence of State Sovereignty is a People living on their own Land and still asserting their Rights to their own Land. Possession is nine-tenths of the Law everywhere around the world! The Kanaka Maoli are still in possession of Hawaii despite the worst efforts by the United States of America to displace them from Hawaii and to extinguish them since at least 1893.

The Kanaka Maoli derive enormous political, economic, psychological, and above-all spiritual powers flowing directly from the fact that they still live on and in their ancestral Homeland of Hawaii—both on the land and at sea. By contrast, the United States of America and its illegal American state of Hawaii know full well that they are mere

Usurpers of the Kanaka Maoli in Hawaii. All the Americans and the other haole in Hawaii bear what we criminal lawyers call "the consciousness of guilt." Everyone knows it!

2. Territory

The second requirement for the restoration of the Kingdom of Hawaii under international law and practice is territory. In the case of Hawaii, the Kanaka Maoli already possess and own the territorial boundaries for the Kingdom of Hawaii as of 1893—both on the land and at sea. Furthermore, the restored Kingdom of Hawaii can qualify as an "archipelagic state" under the 1982 United Nations Law of the Sea Convention (L.O.S.C.), to which it should become a contracting party. Historically, the Kingdom of Hawaii was and still is an archipelagic state. Indeed, as of 1893 other States in the world diplomatically recognized the Kingdom of Hawaii as an archipelagic state by calling it alternatively the Sandwich Islands.

The United States is not a contracting party to the Law of the Sea Convention. But even if the United States were someday to join the L.O.S.C., as an American colony of the United States Hawaii still would not be able to claim the benefits of an "archipelagic state" under the L.O.S.C. Yet, the restored Kingdom of Hawaii can qualify as an archipelagic state under the 1982 Law of the Sea Convention and must publicly claim that status to the L.O.S.C. states parties. The restored Kingdom of Hawaii can also invoke the customary international law doctrines of "historic waters" and "historic bays" to further solidify and extend its claims to territorial Sovereignty over the waters and airspace surrounding the Hawaiian Archipelago beyond the L.O.S.C.

2.1 The Restored Kingdom of Hawaii Will Be an Archipelagic State under the Law of the Sea Convention

The final chapter of this book provides neither the time nor the space to discuss all the ramifications for the restored Kingdom of Hawaii becoming a contracting party to the 1982 U.N. Law of the Sea Convention and claiming its rightful status as an "archipelagic state" thereunder. That task would properly require an entire book in its own right. But briefly put, and only to sketch it out in general and highly impressionistic terms, and certainly not to provide a formal, definitive and technically complete legal analysis here, this is the gist of the analysis:

As an "archipelagic state" under the 1982 Law of the Sea Convention the restored Kingdom of Hawaii would be able to draw what are called "straight baselines" between the outermost points around all of the outermost Islands constituting the Archipelago of Hawaii. According to the L.O.S.C. all the land, waters, resources, subsoil, seabed, and airspace inside those straight baselines would constitute the Sovereign Territory of the restored Kingdom of Hawaii. Furthermore, under the L.O.S.C. the restored Kingdom of Hawaii would also be able to establish a 12 nautical mile Territorial Sea extending outward into the waters from around that straight-baselines system drawn across the outermost points of the outermost Islands of the Hawaiian Archipelago. Within that Territorial Sea the restored Kingdom of Hawaii would have Sovereignty over the waters, the airspace, the seabed, and the subsoil thereof, subject to a right of innocent passage by sea as specified by the L.O.S.C.

As a contracting state party to the Law of the Sea Convention the restored Kingdom of Hawaii can establish a "contiguous zone" extending outward 24 nautical miles from its straight-baselines-system in which it can exercise police powers as specified by the L.O.S.C. In addition, as a contracting state party to the Law of the Sea Convention, the restored Kingdom of Hawaii would be able to establish an Exclusive Economic Zone (E.E.Z.) extending 200 nautical miles beyond its straight-baselines-system. What this E.E.Z. means for the restored Kingdom of Hawaii is succinctly explained in L.O.S.C. article 56:

> Article 56
>
> *Rights, jurisdiction and duties of the coastal State in the exclusive economic zone*
>
> 1. In the exclusive economic zone, the Coastal state has:
>
> (a) sovereign rights for the purpose of exploring and exploiting, conserving and managing the natural resources, whether living or non-living, of the waters superadjacent to the seabed and of the seabed and its subsoil, and with regard to other activities for the economic exploitation and exploration of the zone, such as the production of energy from the water, currents, and winds;
>
> (b) jurisdiction as provided for in the relevant provisions of this Convention with regard to:

> (i) the establishment and use of artificial islands, installations and structures;
>
> (ii) marine scientific research;
>
> (iii) the protection and preservation of the marine environment;
>
> (c) other rights and duties provided for in this Convention.
>
> 2. In exercising its rights and performing its duties under this Convention in the exclusive economic zone, the coastal State shall have due regard to the rights and duties of other States and shall act in a manner compatible with the provisions of this Convention.
>
> 3. The rights set out in this article with respect to the seabed and subsoil shall be exercised in accordance with Part VI.

According to the L.O.S.C., however, the restored Kingdom of Hawaii would have an obligation to prevent the overexploitation of the resources within its E.E.Z.

Furthermore as a contracting party to the Law of the Sea Convention, the restored Kingdom of Hawaii obtains a continental shelf extending a minimum of 200 nautical miles beyond its straight-baselines-system. There the restored Kingdom of Hawaii would have the exclusive right to the exploration and exploitation of the living and non-living natural resources of the water column above and the sea-bed and the subsoil below: oil, gas, minerals, nodules, sedentary species, etc. Finally, the restored Kingdom of Hawaii would also have all the other rights of a contracting state party to the 1982 United Nations Law of the Sea Convention that are too numerous to mention here.[1] These L.O.S.C. rights would include the right to mine the mineral nodules lying on the deep sea-bed of the Pacific Ocean.

In addition, the restored Kingdom of Hawaii could also become a contracting party to the International Convention on Civil Aviation of 1944 (known as the Chicago Convention). This would give the restored Kingdom of Hawaii exclusive sovereignty over the airspace above its land, above its internal waters, and above its territorial sea with no right of innocent passage by aircraft. According to the Law of the Sea Convention, however, there would be a right of archipelagic sea lane passage through and over sea lanes and air routes designated by the restored Kingdom of Hawaii for its "archipelagic waters" as defined by the L.O.S.C.[2] In addition there would also be a right of innocent passage for ships through the "archipelagic waters" of the restored Kingdom of Hawaii as defined and specified by the L.O.S.C.

No point would be served by detailing all the implications that would arise for passage by aircraft and ships should the restored Kingdom of Hawaii become a contracting party to the Chicago Convention and the Law of the Sea Convention. Suffice it to say here that the restored Kingdom of Hawaii would enjoy exceedingly more rights, benefits, privileges, and protections than the illegal American State of Hawaii does today on the seas, in the seas, under the seas, and in the airspace above the seas. This proposition holds true even if the United States were to become a contracting party to the Law of the Sea Convention.

Basically the United States sold out, sacrificed, short-changed, and undermined the historical claims and interests of Hawaii and the Kanaka Maoli when it negotiated the Law of the Sea Convention in order to promote and advance its own imperial designs and rapacious desires around the oceans and the shores of the world.[3] No surprise there! But all the more reason for the Kanaka Maoli to restore the Kingdom of Hawaii, and then to claim their rightful place in the sun as an "archipelagic state" under the Law of the Sea Convention and beyond.

2.2: The Economy of the Restored Kingdom of Hawaii

With this vast area of fertile land, waters, fisheries, continental shelf, seabed, subsoil, oil, gas, nodules, minerals, wind, waves, sun, centrally located airspace and sea lanes in the very middle of the Pacific Ocean, transit servicing charges etc., the restored Kingdom of Hawaii would have more than enough natural wealth and physical resources to render the Kanaka Maoli economically self-sufficient and indeed prosperous and certainly independent of the colonial, genocidal, racist, and predatory economic tentacles of the United States of America and those of other powerful States in the Pacific such as Japan and China. This restored Kingdom of Hawaii would have all of the economic wealth and natural resources necessary for the Kanaka Maoli by themselves to ensure their own economic survival and prosperity as a cognizable People for the benefit of their Children and their Children's Children *ad infinitum* for the rest of their historical existence on this earth. The Kanaka Maoli would have thus ensured their own economic future and their own physical existence. The restored Kingdom of Hawaii could become the Switzerland of the Pacific Ocean instead of Kanakamaolilandustan for the amusement of the haole tourists.

The economy of the restored Kingdom of Hawaii no longer need be dependent upon tourism by the American Yankees and the other haole. The Kanaka Maoli can permit, regulate, and control haole tourism to the extent desired for their own economic benefit and in whatever manner they deem fit in accordance with respect for their customs, and traditions, and heritage. This is certainly not the case today when the Yankees and the other haole conduct haole tourism for their own economic benefit and in gross disrespect for and distortion of Kanaka Maoli customs, traditions, and religion.

In the restored Kingdom of Hawaii the Yankees and other haole will no longer be able to exploit the Kanaka Maoli in order to make a Yankee Buck from haole tourists. In fact the Kingdom of Hawaii can set up its own central bank with a money-issuing capacity to ensure its control over its own economy and development. Among other things, establishing its own currency would make the haole tourists convert their haole currencies into the Kanaka Maoli currency. The Kanaka Maoli can make a profit on the currency conversion—both the rate and a fee. A currency independent of the Yankee Buck will provide an additional source of revenue-creating powers for the restored Kingdom of Hawaii that the Kanaka Maoli can use for their exclusive benefit to develop their economy. A new currency for the restored Kingdom of Hawaii will liberate the Kanaka Maoli from the colonial, racist, and genocidal—and declining—Yankee Buck, Wall Street banksters, and the piratical U.S. Federal Reserve.

Generally put, the citizens of the restored Kingdom of Hawaii would pay no taxes to the United States government unless they worked in America or were dual-nationals or derived some other source of income from there. The restored Kingdom of Hawaii could negotiate and conclude a Tax Treaty with the United States in order to avoid double-taxation for their respective nationals, whether natural persons or businesses. In this manner, the enormous American colonial tax burden that the Kanaka Maoli currently suffer from would be lifted from their shoulders. Instead, all taxes in Hawaii would be paid to the restored Kingdom of Hawaii for the benefit of the Kanaka Maoli and its other citizens and not that of the Yankees and the other haole.

2.3: The Restored Kingdom of Hawaii Could Be Neutral, Neutralized, Non-aligned, and Demilitarized

The restored Kingdom of Hawaii could proclaim that it is a Permanently Neutral and Neutralized State; that it is and shall remain Non-aligned from any military Alliance of States; and that it will be a permanently Demilitarized State like Costa Rica. Therefore, the restored Kingdom of Hawaii would maintain no military or paramilitary forces and thus the Kanaka Maoli would not have to pay for these either. These arrangements can be approved and guaranteed by the United Nations Security Council by means of the Security Council adopting a U.N. Charter Chapter 7 Resolution that would be binding upon every state in the world. To be sure, the restored Kingdom of Hawaii would have to maintain an effective Coast Guard and Civil Air Patrol in order to police its extensive waters and shores for the twin purposes of exercising its rights and discharging its obligations under the Law of the Sea Convention and the Chicago Civil Aviation Convention. This would free the Kanaka Maoli from having to pay their currently American-imposed colonial quotas for the outrageous U.S. war/defense/national-security-state tax burdens and the astronomical U.S. national debt. In the likely event that the United States government attempts to allocate and to impose what it deems to be a "fair share" of the U.S. national debt upon the restored Kingdom of Hawaii, the Kanaka Maoli can invoke the customary international law doctrine of "odious debt" in order to repudiate all of it right down to the very last Yankee penny.

I see no point here continuing to analyze the additional economic benefits that would be gained for the Kanaka Maoli by restoring their Kingdom of Hawaii: e.g., free trade zones; international banking and financial institutions; tax-incentivized development zones to encourage high-tech enterprises, pharmaceuticals, biomedical research, power generation by sun and wind and waves, and other cutting-edge ventures. The list can go on. The restored Kingdom of Hawaii should commission a detailed study by independent experts of the economies of Switzerland, Singapore, Dubai, and Malaysia, inter alia. Then the restored Kingdom of Hawaii can decide for itself what elements of these prosperous economies are most suitable and beneficial for the Kanaka Maoli themselves.

3. Government

The third requirement for the restored Kingdom of Hawaii under international law and practice is a functioning government—one that is functioning both internationally and domestically. This brings the analysis to the fundamental dilemma that confronts the Kanaka Maoli today. The Kanaka Maoli already have the 1893 Kingdom of Hawaii that only needs to be restored. This can be done at the forthcoming Convention when the Kanaka Maoli there vote for its Restoration. But then that restored Kingdom of Hawaii will need to have a government that can incarnate and represent their State and conduct its affairs—both internationally and domestically. Therefore, it is my most respectful advice to those Kanaka Maoli who attend the forthcoming Convention that they vote: (1) first, to restore the Kingdom of Hawaii; and then (2) second, to establish a Provisional Government of National Unity (P.G.N.U.) for their restored Kingdom of Hawaii.

Today there are a plethora of different Kanaka Maoli Ohana, Sovereignty groups, organizations, movements, and leaders who all in good faith and conscience have already drafted or resurrected or established Charters, Constitutions, and Governments etc. that certainly represent definite segments of strong opinion and felt support among the Kanaka Maoli themselves. It is not my intention here to criticize any of these Kanaka Maoli Ohana, Sovereignty groups, organizations, leaders, respective memberships, Charters, Constitutions, or Governments, etc., but rather to approve and applaud them all. They all constitute preliminary steps toward Independence and are thus most valuable.

Yet in my professional opinion what the Kanaka Maoli really need to do now is to establish a **Provisional Government of National Unity** (P.G.N.U.) that represents them all while in the process of voting for the restoration of the Kingdom of Hawaii at the forthcoming Convention. All the disparate Kanaka Maoli Ohana, Sovereignty groups, organizations, movements, leaders, memberships, and governments must come together in order to create and then to support this Provisional Government of National Unity for the restored Kingdom of Hawaii. This can and must be done by those Kanaka Maoli who attend the forthcoming Convention. In this manner, the Kanaka Maoli would be "organizing themselves" as called for by American Hawaiian Colonial Act 195 (2011), but certainly not in the way that its drafters either intended or anticipated or desired. Once again, the Kanaka Maoli can and must perform political jiu-jitsu against the Yankees and the other haole by means of international law at the forthcoming Convention by voting to restore the Kingdom of Hawaii, and then creating a Provisional Government of National Unity for it.

3.1: The Precedent of Palestine and the Palestinians

In strong support for this advice, I respectfully submit for consideration by the Kanaka Maoli the precedent set by the Palestinians creating their State of Palestine by means of international law. During the past quarter-century the entire world has witnessed and for the most part supported one amazing historical example of nation-state-building by means of public international law that has worked strikingly well and is now on the verge of ultimate success: The creation of the State of Palestine by the Palestinians.

Starting in June of 1987, I served as Legal Advisor to the Palestine Liberation Organization (P.L.O.) and to its Chairman, Yasser Arafat, on the Palestinian Declaration of Independence of 15 November 1988 that included therein the creation of the State of Palestine. It was my idea. I had publicly proposed this initiative to the Palestinians and the world at large while speaking at United Nations Headquarters in New York as their invited guest and speaker in June of 1987 in order to commemorate the 20th Anniversary of the so-called Six Day War.

I am not going to repeat here the 25+-year history of Palestinian nation-state-building by means of public international law. That story can be found related sequentially in three of my books: *Palestine, Palestinians and International Law* (2003); *Breaking All the Rules* (2008); and *The Palestinian Right of Return under International Law* (2011). How the Palestinians created their own State of Palestine by means of public international law from when I first proposed the idea to them while speaking before the United Nations Organization in June of 1987 right up to their submission of their Application for full-fledged State Membership for Palestine to the United Nations Organization on 23 September 2011 is chronicled in the pages of these three books together with the related legal documentation and argumentation for their unilateral right to do so.

Theirs was a Unilateral Declaration of Independence: a U.D.I. This is exactly what I am recommending that the Kanaka Maoli unilaterally do at the forthcoming Convention. Only for the Kanaka Maoli it should be a Unilateral Declaration of Restoration: Restoration of the Kingdom of Hawaii. U.D.R.

In a nutshell and to make this quarter-century-long history of nation-state-building by the Palestinians by means of international law very short: Today the State of Palestine is recognized bilaterally and de jure by about 133 other States out of the present 193 Member States of the United Nations Organization. Palestine has State Membership in U.N.E.S.C.O., a United Nations Specialized Agency, among other international organizations. On 29 November 2012 the United Nations General Assembly voted to make Palestine a U.N. Observer State along the lines of what Switzerland had been before it joined the United Nations Organization as a full-fledged Member State in 2002.[4]

I advised the Palestinians in June of 1987 to obtain State membership for Palestine in the United Nations Organization and counseled them on how to do it. Today the votes in the U.N. General Assembly to admit Palestine as a full-fledged U.N. Member State are already there among the 193 U.N. Member States. The only thing that has kept Palestine from becoming a full-fledged U.N. Member State is the threat of a veto by the United States government at the United Nations Security Council. To counteract that, I devised a strategy whereby the Palestinians can circumvent this threatened U.S. veto at the U.N. Security Council and have Palestine admitted as a full-fledged U.N. Member State by means of having the U.N. General Assembly invoke the General Assembly's Uniting for Peace Resolution of 1950. It is only a question of time and timing. The future of Palestine and the Palestinians is now in their own hands thanks to public international law and of course primarily because of their own resistance and iron will in pursuit of their right to self-determination, which has drawn widespread international support. To be sure, the Kanaka Maoli have demonstrated their own iron will for self-determination, and widespread international support for the restored Kingdom of Hawaii resulting from it is the likelihood for the Kanaka Maoli as well. It is now high time for the Kanaka Maoli to put international law to work for themselves!

The Kanaka Maoli can and must do the same as the Palestinians by voting to restore their Kingdom of Hawaii at this forthcoming Convention. But under public international law, their State must have a Government. The same situation confronted the Palestinians in June 1987 when I first began to advise them on their nation-state-building process by means of international law. First the Palestinians needed unilaterally to declare Independence and then second to create a State. Then third, the Palestinians needed to create a Government for their State.

So in the drafting of their 15 November 1988 Declaration of Independence that created the State of Palestine, I also advised the Palestinians that they must establish therein a Government for the State of Palestine. Therefore, I advised the Palestinians that their 15 November 1988 Declaration of Independence must: (1) first, declare Independence; (2) second, create the State of Palestine; and then (3), third, determine that the Executive Committee of the Palestine Liberation Organization shall serve as the "Provisional Government" for the State of Palestine. "Provisional" meant and still means today provisional until Israel, the illegal belligerent power that is occupying Palestine withdraws from and evacuates Palestine. And then the Palestinians can organize free, fair, and democratic elections of their own volition without duress and coercion perpetrated upon them by Israel in order to establish the Republic of Palestine with their own freely determined Constitution for it.

So it was done! Today the P.L.O. Executive Committee still serves as the Provisional Government for the State of Palestine after 25+ years. It is the P.L.O. Executive Committee serving in its capacity under public international law as the Provisional Government for the State of Palestine that has acted internationally for the past 25+ years to bring into fruition the State of Palestine and its ineluctable full-fledged State membership in the United Nations Organization as well as Palestine's de jure diplomatic recognition and relations with about 133 other states out of 193 United Nations Member States together with Palestine's U.N. Observer State Status. Large numbers of other States in the world today deal with and recognize the State of Palestine on a de facto basis, including most States of Europe. Someday soon almost every state in the world will officially recognize the State of Palestine and establish de jure diplomatic relations with it.

The Kanaka Maoli can and must do the same for their 1893 Kingdom of Hawaii which they can restore at the forthcoming Convention. But like the Palestinians, the Kanaka Maoli need to establish a Government for their restored Kingdom of Hawaii. Hence my advice is that when the Kanaka Maoli present at the forthcoming Convention vote to restore the Kingdom of Hawaii, they must also set up a Provisional Government of National Unity (P.G.N.U.) for that State. Just like the Palestinians did in their 15 November 1988 Declaration of Independence for the State of Palestine.

Except that for Hawaii it should be a Declaration of Restoration for the Kingdom of Hawaii—and not a Declaration of Independence. The Kanaka Maoli already have their 1893 Kingdom of Hawaii that still exists today as a subject of international law and thus which only needs to be restored—unlike the Palestinians who needed to create their State in the first place when I first advised them to do so in June of 1987. For that very reason, the task of nation-state-building by means of international law that confronts the Kanaka Maoli today is far less daunting than the task of nation-state-building by means of international law that confronted the Palestinians and me in June of 1987.

Back then there were many different Palestinian groups, organizations, factions, and leaders. Eventually the late P.L.O Chairman Yasser Arafat and his organization Fatah were able to pull them all together, and by the processes of debate, argument, consensus, voting, non-violence and public international law declared their Independence on 15 November 1988, creating thereby the State of Palestine, and then set up therein the P.L.O. Executive Committee to serve as the Provisional Government for the State of Palestine. This Palestinian State and its provisional Government represented and included Palestinians living in Occupied Palestine as well as and especially the massive Palestinian Diaspora dispersed all over the world who were forced to leave their homes in Palestine by Israel in 1948. Today, after twenty-five years of hard work, all Palestinians living around the world are now singing from the same Hymnal of nation-state-building by means of international law via the United Nations Organization.

3.2: Building the Restored Kingdom of Hawaii from the Ground and the Seas of Hawaii on Up and Out

So from my professional experience and perspective, the Kanaka Maoli need to create a Provisional Government of National Unity for their restored Kingdom of Hawaii that pulls together all the different Ohana, Sovereignty groups, organizations, movements, and memberships and leaders, and charters, constitutions and governments that can represent all the Kanaka Maoli in Hawaii and around the world in all of their multifarious capacities and constituencies and ways of life. This Provisional Government of National Unity must speak for as many Kanaka Maoli as possible, including and especially those Kanaka Maoli living in their enforced Diaspora—just like the Palestinians did in their 15 November 1988 Declaration of Independence. It must proceed to construct their State from the ground and the seas of Hawaii on up and out among the Kanaka Maoli themselves in Hawaii and among those Kanaka Maoli scattered around the world in their Diaspora—*despite* the illegal U.S. belligerent and colonial and military occupation of Hawaii. Just like the Palestinians have done in Palestine even while living under the illegal belligerent, colonial, and military occupation of Palestine by Israel.

Similarly, the P.G.N.U. must set out to provide education, health care, housing, clothing, food, dispute-settlement, justice, jobs, etc. for all Kanaka Maoli as best they can while living under the illegal U.S. belligerent and colonial and military occupation of Hawaii. The Palestinians have done this while living under the most brutal belligerent colonial and military occupation by Israel as well as for their Diaspora. The Kanaka Maoli can and must do the same in Hawaii living under the most brutal American belligerent colonial and military occupation as well as for their Diaspora. This process can and must be commenced by the Kanaka Maoli establishing a Provisional Government of National Unity for their restored Kingdom of Hawaii at the forthcoming Convention.

3.3: Kanaka Maoli Nation-State-Building Must Be by Means of the Spirit of Aloha, *Satyagraha*, Non-violent Civil Resistance, and International Law

I also want to make it perfectly clear here that I am not advocating violence to the Kanaka Maoli. Violence would be inconsistent with and contrary to the innate Kanaka Maoli Spirit of Aloha, and thus counterproductive and bound to fail. Rather, I am advocating Mahatma Gandhi's *Satyagraha:* Truth-Force, non-violent civil resistance. Gandhi was a man of the East—not the haole Yankee West.

Non-violent civil resistance is fully consistent with and embodies the Kanaka Maoli Spirit of Aloha.[5] Since Gandhi and his *Satyagraha* threw out the tottering British Empire from the entire Indian sub-continent, then certainly the Kanaka Maoli by means of *Satyagraha* and non-violent civil resistance and the Spirit of Aloha and public international law can throw out the tottering American Empire from Hawaii. The Americans and the other haole in Hawaii are possessed by their congenital "consciousness of guilt" for stealing Hawaii from the Kanaka Maoli. By contrast, the Kanaka Maoli possess and must now manifest their congenital Consciousness of Ownership of Hawaii.

Today both sides know and understand their antithetically opposed psychological and spiritual powers and lack thereof in the case of the Americans and the other haole together with their interactional dynamics. Gandhi and the British did too. That is why Gandhi won and the British lost. That will also be why the Kanaka Maoli will win and the Yankees will lose. Gandhi wielded *Satyagraha* from the Indians' moral and psychological and spiritual "high ground" against the British. The Kanaka Maoli must likewise employ *Satyagraha*, non-violent civil resistance, the Spirit of Aloha, and public international law from their moral and psychological and spiritual "high ground" against the Yankees and the other haole in Hawaii. The net result will be the same and for the same reasons: Independence!

3.4 Not in Court

The Kanaka Maoli are not going to get the Kingdom of Hawaii restored by going to Court and asking some Court to give it to them. Keanu Sai and I already tried to do so by going to the U.S. Supreme Court for that express purpose as already explained in Chapter 4 of this book. At the time I felt that even though the odds were quite high against us, as a matter of principle the effort had to be made at the United States Supreme Court to restore the Kingdom of Hawaii, and especially in order to commemorate the 100th anniversary of the illegal annexation of the Kingdom of Hawaii by the United States and its subsequent illegal belligerent, colonial, and military occupation of Hawaii. Nevertheless, as explained in Chapter 4, even the United States Supreme Court treated the 1893 Kingdom of Hawaii as a de jure sovereign nation state that still exists today. The Kanaka Maoli themselves must now build upon what Keanu and I had achieved at the U.S. Supreme Court.

Moreover, based upon my experience as a successful Litigator before the International Court of Justice in The Hague for the Republic of Bosnia and Herzegovina during Yugoslavia's genocidal war of extermination against the Bosnians, the World Court is not going to restore the Kingdom of Hawaii either. Rather, the Kanaka Maoli will have to do this for themselves and by their own hands, and hearts, and minds, and souls. Just as the Palestinians have done. Then the restored Kingdom of Hawaii can someday sue the United States before the International Court of Justice for all the damages America has inflicted upon the Kanaka Maoli and Hawaii since at least 1893. Just as the Palestinians have now publicly threatened to sue Israel before the International Court of Justice acting on the basis of my legal advice to them. The Kanaka Maoli's day at the World Court shall come too!

3.5: The Restoration of the Republic of Lithuania by the Lithuanians

To be more precise both legally and historically: The Kanaka Maoli must do what the Lithuanians have already successfully done. As explained in the Introduction to this book, the Lithuanians successfully restored the Republic of Lithuania on 11 March 1990 after 50 years of a most brutal, racist, colonial, and genocidal invasion, occupation, mass deportation, and annexation of their Homeland by the infamous Stalin and the mighty Soviet Union. I have already discussed the legal work I did for the Republic of Lithuania and its heroic President Vytautas Landsbergis starting in January of 1991 in order to help them restore the Republic of Lithuania in the Introduction to this book. So I am not going to repeat any of that analysis here. But the Lithuanians restored the Republic of Lithuania and threw out the tottering Soviet Empire from Lithuania. So likewise the Kanaka Maoli can and must vote to restore the Kingdom of Hawaii with a Provisional Government of National Unity for it at the forthcoming Convention, and then proceed to throw out the tottering American Empire from Hawaii.

Indeed, the United States of America and its Empire around the world might very well collapse for the exact same reasons that the Union of Soviet Socialist Republics and its Empire over the Warsaw Pact states of Eastern Europe collapsed in late 1991. The Kanaka Maoli must now plan and prepare for that momentous day. So at the forthcoming Convention the Kanaka Maoli must (1) vote to restore the Kingdom of Hawaii, and then (2) create the Provisional Government of National Unity for it. Just like the Lithuanians restored the Republic of Lithuania in early 1990 before the unexpected collapse of the Soviet Union and its Empire in late 1991.

History very well might repeat itself here. The United States and its American Empire are well beyond the point of "imperial overstretch." After September 11, 2001, the American Yankees decided to go for broke in their quest for worldwide domination. "Whom the gods would destroy, they first make mad."

Today the restored Republic of Lithuania is a full-fledged Member State of the United Nations Organization. The Kanaka Maoli can and must work for the same U.N. membership for the restored Kingdom of Hawaii. The Kanaka Maoli must begin their existential quest toward obtaining full-fledged U.N. State Membership for the restored Kingdom of Hawaii at this forthcoming Convention. But the Kanaka Maoli require a Provisional Government of National Unity for it in order to accomplish that goal. No United Nations Member State has ever been destroyed.

4. Capacity to Conduct International Relations

The fourth and final requirement for the restoration of the Kingdom of Hawaii is the capacity to conduct international relations. The Provisional Government of National Unity must construct the restored Kingdom of Hawaii from the ground and the seas of Hawaii on up and out among all the Kanaka Maoli both in Hawaii and around the world in their Diaspora in the manner previously explained. But in addition to this task and at the same time, the P.G.N.U. must also seek and obtain diplomatic recognition and treaty relations from other States and International Organizations all over the World, including and especially from the United Nations Organization and its Specialized Agencies like U.N.E.S.C.O.

The P.G.N.U. must pick up and take off from where the Kingdom of Hawaii left off in 1893. The P.G.N.U. must re-establish diplomatic relations and treaty relations with all those states and their respective governments that the Kingdom of Hawaii had diplomatic relations and treaty relations with as of 1893. The P.G.N.U. must contact those governments and request the revival of the presently only dormant diplomatic relations and treaty relations that had already existed with those States as of 1893. The P.G.N.U. must do the same with the Universal Postal Union where the Kingdom of Hawaii was and still is a full-fledged member state.

The P.G.N.U. must argue to these states with which it had enjoyed relations in 1893 that the restored Kingdom of Hawaii is the lawful continuation of the 1893 Kingdom of Hawaii whose existence as a subject under international law was never legally terminated by the United States in 1893. *Ex iniuria ius non oritur!* Right does not arise from injury!

Keep in mind, the P.G.N.U. is simply asking these governments to revive and to resume diplomatic relations and treaty relations that their respective states had already established with the Kingdom of Hawaii as of 1893, which at this time are only dormant. They have lain in a state of suspended animation under international law since 1893 and so only need to be revived and resumed, and not created in the first place. The latter task is a far more difficult job under international law and practice—which the Palestinians have nevertheless successfully surmounted. A fortiori and ditto for the restored Republic of Lithuania.

Eventually, the P.G.N.U. can extend these processes of establishing diplomatic relations and treaty relations to states and governments that did not have diplomatic relations or treaty relations with the Kingdom of Hawaii as of 1893. The diplomatic recognition by these post-1893 states can be either de facto (in practice) or de jure (in law) to begin with. In other words, when these foreign governments start dealing with the P.G.N.U.—for whatever reason and in whatever manner— that would constitute de facto diplomatic recognition of the restored Kingdom of Hawaii by these post-1893 states.

The establishment of de facto diplomatic recognition and commencing the negotiation of treaty relations with these post-1893 states and governments can then be incrementally deepened and improved by the P.G.N.U. over time. The Palestinians started with de facto recognition for their State of Palestine. The Palestinian processes of nation-state-building by means of international law incrementally evolved into de jure recognition of the State of Palestine by the United Nations General Assembly and 133 states out of 193 U.N. member states over a period of 25 years. A quarter-century is the approximate time-frame the Kanaka Maoli are looking at now for the restored Kingdom of Hawaii to join the United Nations Organization as a full-fledged member state unless the United States and its Empire collapse sooner than that. This epic event very well might occur sooner rather than later, and would forward the process.

The Kanaka Maoli can and must do the same as the Palestinians at the United Nations for the Kingdom of Hawaii restored at the forthcoming Convention. But that State will need the Convention also to establish a Provisional Government of National Unity in order to conduct these international relations going forward—to obtain de facto and then de jure diplomatic recognition of the restored Kingdom of Hawaii by other governments and international organizations; as well as to enter into treaty relations with these respective governments and with international organizations by becoming a member state. The mere fact that the P.G.N.U. has started to engage in these diplomatic activities and treaty initiatives will then fulfill the fourth and final requirement for Statehood under international law and practice for the restored Kingdom of Hawaii: the capacity to conduct international relations. Again and nevertheless: the Kanaka Maoli will need a P.G.N.U. to begin with. Hence, those Kanaka Maoli who attend the forthcoming Convention must vote to restore the Kingdom of Hawaii, and then create a Provisional Government of National Unity for it.

Conclusion

Obviously this is a medium-term agenda calling for about 25+ years of hard work based upon the successful precedent of nation-state-building of Palestine by the Palestinians by means of using international law. The American Yankee problem has been in Hawaii since 1893 and even before then, going back at least to the so-called Bayonet Constitution of 1887, which is entitled to no legal significance whatsoever under international law or otherwise. *Ex iniuria ius non oritur!* Right does not arise from injury!

The American Yankee problem that afflicts Hawaii and the

Kanaka Maoli today is not going to be resolved tomorrow. But look at the tremendous progress the Palestinians have made in just 25 years. A quarter-century is just the blink of an eye in the long and distinguished history of the Kanaka Maoli in Hawaii. By contrast, America is just a speck in the eye of the historic and longstanding Kanaka Maoli who need to expel it from Hawaii. **Yankee go home!**

I am not sure if I will be walking on the face of this earth twenty-five years from now when Hawaii is on the verge of full-fledged state membership in the United Nations Organization as my clients and friends Palestine and the Palestinians are today. Insha'Allah I shall be there for that glorious day! **Free Hawaii!**

ENDNOTES

1 *See generally* Louis B. Sohn & Kristen Gustafson, The Law of the Sea (1984).

2 *See* Major George W. Ash, *1982 Convention on the Law of the Sea – Its Impact on Air Law*, 26 A.F.L. Rev. 35 (1987). "Archipelagic waters" is a L.O.S.C. term of art that is not necessary to explain here for the purpose of this analysis.

3 *See* Nancy Barron, *Archipelagos and Archipelagic States Under UNCLOS III: No Special Treatment for Hawaii*, 4 Hastings Int'l & Comp. L. Rev. 509 (1992).

4 *See* Dennis Bernstein, *An Interview with Professor Francis Boyle*, Counterpunch.org, Dec. 4, 2012.

5 Francis A. Boyle, Defending Civil Resistance Under International Law (Transnational Publishers Inc.: 1987) (Special Edition For Pro Se Protestors: 1988).

CONCLUSION

On June 20, 2014, the haole Obama administration's Department of the "Interior" promulgated *Proposed Rules: Procedures for Reestablishing a Government-to-Government Relationship with the Native Hawaiian Community.* By means of this document, the Obama administration made it patently clear that it fully intends to reduce the mighty Kanaka Maoli —the Sons and the Daughters of the Great King Kamehameha and the Great Queen Liliuokalani—to nothing more than an Indian Tribe with an Indian Reservation located on a Bantustan somewhere on the Islands of Hawaii for the benefit of resolving the Kanaka Maoli "situation" for the haoles and eliminating any possible uncertainty as to title to lands and resources. Hawaii is obviously not "interior" to the United States. Any objective observer could easily determine that basic fact by merely glancing at a globe of the world.

These 6/20/2014 haole U.S. "Interior" Department "proposed rules" are mean, nasty, vicious, cruel, brutal, condescending, racist, and genocidal against the Kanaka Maoli. So I am not going to dignify these "proposed rules" with any type of extended analysis here. The Kanaka Maoli do not need any type of "assistance" or "support" from the U.S. Federal Department of the "Interior," an agency of their current occupying power. When has the U.S. Federal Government ever had the best interests of the Kanaka Maoli in mind?

The Kanaka Maoli must not work with or cooperate with the racist and genocidal haole U.S. Department of the "Interior" or accede to either Hawaii or themselves being incorporated into another state, the United States of America. Contrary to these "proposed domestic rules" of the U.S. belligerent occupier who has already admitted its wrongfulness by means of its 1993 Apology for having done so, it is the Kanaka Maoli right of self-determination under international law that is at stake here, trumping the United States federal "laws" and responding to the situation now created by the fact of that 1993 Apology and admission of the illegitimacy of its occupation. The Kanaka Maoli can and must take their own future and that of Hawaii into their own hands. The Kanaka Maoli must not permit the U.S. Federal Government and its puppet government known as the American "state" of Hawaii to determine their fate and that of their beloved Hawaii.

It is now obvious for the entire world to see that the illegal haole American state of Hawaii and the haole United States Federal Government that illegally occupies Hawaii have been conspiring together hand-in-hand for quite some time on their racist and genocidal scheme to reduce the mighty Kanaka Maoli into nothing more than an Indian Tribe that occupies nothing more than an Indian Reservation on a Bantustan located somewhere on the Islands of Hawaii, leaving the exercise of sovereignty, and the benefits to be derived from use of the land and resources in the hands of the haoles. Consequently, this is an historical moment of utmost existential danger for the Kanaka Maoli and their beloved Hawaii: the haole American "final solution" for the Kanaka Maoli themselves and the bantustanization of Hawaii. This is a U.S. freight train carrying cattle cars with the Kanaka Maoli standing in them that has already left the station and is now barreling down the tracks towards a rendezvous with their own Auschwitz. It must be stopped! Better yet: It must be derailed!

How best to do that?

It is my most respectful advice that all eligible Kanaka Maoli attend the upcoming Convention, and while there vote to restore the 1893 Kingdom of Hawaii, and then establish a Provisional Government of National Unity for it.

Next, this Provisional Government of National Unity must immediately launch a full-court-press all over the world to obtain either de facto or de jure diplomatic recognition for the restored Kingdom of Hawaii as a sovereign and independent Kanaka Maoli nation state. I have already described why and how this can be done in chapter 6 of this book. So I will not repeat any of that analysis here.

With respect to "reestablishing a government-to-government relationship" with the United States Federal Government as called for by these haole "interior" proposed rules, the Provisional Government of National Unity must seek to obtain formal de jure diplomatic recognition for the restored Kingdom of Hawaii directly from President Obama himself—not from the racist and genocidal haole U.S. Department of the "Interior." According to Article 2, Section 3 of the United States Constitution the President of the United States has the power and the authority to "receive Ambassadors and other public Ministers." The United States Supreme Court has consistently interpreted this clause of the United States Constitution to mean that the President of the United States has the exclusive and plenary power to recognize foreign states.

This means that President Obama can extend formal diplomatic recognition to the restored Kingdom of Hawaii as the de jure independent nation state for the Kanaka Maoli without any approval by the United States Congress or by the United States Courts or by anyone else for that matter. This is exactly what the Kanaka Maoli want and deserve from the United States Government for their restored Kingdom of Hawaii with its Provisional Government of National Unity: *restitutio in integrum*, restoring the situation to what it was in 1893 before the illegal overthrow of the Kingdom of Hawaii by the United States Government. That is the type of "government-to-government relationship" that "the Native Hawaiian Community" can and must seek to "reestablish" with the United States Federal Government.

All by himself, President Obama can finally and definitively rectify the grievous historical injustice that the United States of America inflicted upon the Kingdom of Hawaii and the Kanaka Maoli in 1893 by today extending formal de jure diplomatic recognition to the Kingdom of Hawaii and its Provisional Government of National Unity. After all, President Obama was born in Hawaii. President Obama owes this act of Restoration to the Kanaka Maoli whose beloved Hawaii birthed and nurtured him.

But if he fails to do so, the above-mentioned process in its entirety will have clarified the illegitimacy of the U.S.-imposed relationship between the United States government and the occupied Kanaka Maoli Kingdom of Hawaii, and facilitate Kanaka Maoli pursuit of their international legal right to self-determination on the international level. No matter what President Obama ultimately might do, the Kanaka Maoli must deal with him directly as the Head of State of the United States of America, not with the racist and genocidal U.S. Federal Department of the Interior and the U.S. government's longstanding Bureau of Indian Affairs that serves as the permanent and functioning graveyard for so many extinct American Indian Nations of past history. The Kanaka Maoli do not want to become yet another one of their victims. In any event, the destiny of the Kanaka Maoli and of Hawaii resides in their own hands.

Free Hawaii!

INDEX

Printed in Dunstable, United Kingdom

88177732R00111